DOUBLEDAY
CELEBRATES
100 YEARS OF
EXCELLENCE

DR. JANE GREER

&

MARGERY D. ROSEN

Doubleday

NEW YORK LONDON

TORONTO SYDNEY AUCKLAND

HOW COULD YOU DO THIS TO ME?

Learning to

Trust After Betrayal

PUBLISHED BY DOUBLEDAY
a division of Bantam Doubleday Dell Publishing Group, Inc.
1540 Broadway, New York, New York 10036

DOUBLEDAY and the portrayal of an anchor with a dolphin
are trademarks of Doubleday, a division of Bantam Doubleday Dell
Publishing Group, Inc.

Book design by Dana Leigh Treglia

Library of Congress Cataloging-in-Publication Data
Greer, Jane, 1951–
How could you do this to me? : learning to trust after betrayal /
Jane Greer with Margery D. Rosen. — 1st ed.
p.   cm.
Includes bibliographical references.
1. Trust (Psychology)   2. Betrayal—Psychological aspects.
3. Interpersonal relations.   I. Rosen, Margery D.   II. Title.
BF575.T7G74   1997
158'.2—dc20   96-23189
                                                                      CIP

1   3   5   7   9   10   8   6   4   2

TO MY HUSBAND, MARC,

FOR NEVER MISSING THE MOMENT

AUTHOR'S NOTE

As a psychotherapist, I consider it my first priority to safeguard the confidentiality of my patients and interview subjects. In the interest of protecting their privacy, I have changed the names of all persons mentioned in the book, except the psychologists and other theorists quoted. I have also altered the details of people's lives—their professions, family backgrounds, and other potentially identifying circumstances.

ACKNOWLEDGMENTS

I have had the opportunity to meet and work with a variety of people through my practice, the seminars I teach, and the television shows on which I appear. They have shared their stories of betrayal, their hurt, and pain, hoping to understand what they went through and, most important, to heal. Their experiences are the foundation of this book, and I want to thank them for letting me into their lives. My hope is that I provided some shelter from the storm and some guidance that can protect them from now on.

No project can be completed without the support of many. I want to express my deepest appreciation and gratitude to the following people for making this book possible.

Margery Rosen is the quintessential writing partner. Her enthusiasm and belief in this project fueled it from the start; her zest, spirit, and tenacity sustained it; and her wealth of talent made this book a labor of love.

Without my agent, Geri Thoma, whose conviction of "once more with feeling" prevailed, this project would not have happened.

My editor, Lori Lipsky, gave her enthusiastic response and commitment to this book, from the get-go to the finish.

My colleague and treasured friend for all seasons, Dr. Josie Palleja, is an eternal part of my heart and family. Thanks for your unbounding love, friendship, steady nurturance, encouragement, and constant gems of wisdom that see me through every facet of my life.

I also thank my forever friend Kathy Pomerantz, for sharing your "technicolor" love and laughter. Whenever it counts most, you're always there. You are my true "cielo" blue pal. What would I do without you?

Louise DuArt, my dearest buddy and All-Star Therapy partner, thanks for being in the right place at the right time, and bringing your love and friendship into my life. Here's to a lifetime of "get the bags."

Thanks also to my friend Lesley Krupnik. With your incredible finishing touch, you always help me pull everything together. You are my guardian angel.

A heartfelt thank you as well to:

My dear friend and colleague Dr. Sonya Rhodes; you remain an inspiration.

Charles Cook, for your trusted friendship and for always taking the time to care.

Laura Merini, for the opportunity to appear on the television program that gave birth to the idea of this book.

Roz Linder, for your generous help with shared experiences.

I can't begin to thank my family enough. My brother, for giving me a lifelong musical medley of love. Because of you, I can always cross that bridge when "we" come to it.

My Aunt Ruth. Your presence is always with me.

My parents' unconditional love and support make it all possible. Thanks, Mom, for giving me strength through all your encouragement; for being with me through every success; for seeing me through every defeat; and for making me who I am today through all your love. Dad, thanks for teaching me that it pays to never take no for an answer, never give up, and most especially for always coming through for me.

And finally, I thank my life partner in love and work, Marc Snowman, for your "belief," for your generosity of heart, for a million shared laughs that smooth the rough edges, for your unwavering support on all fronts, and for always being there to help me find my way.

CONTENTS

Contents

Contents

SECTION III

The Fallout from Betrayal

129

Contents

HOW COULD YOU

DO THIS TO ME?

INTRODUCTION

Time and again, people you love, respect, and count on—lovers, family, friends, or colleagues—behave in ways that wound you deeply, shake your faith in them and in yourself, and tear at the fabric of your relationships. It's not easy for anyone to live with betrayal, large or small. Though you may understand it intellectually, emotionally you are scalded by the broken trust.

Mention the word *trust* or *betrayal,* and most people think immediately of sexual infidelity. While an affair is certainly a devastating betrayal of trust, it is only one of the many types of betrayals I will deal with in this book. Some betrayals are deliberate; others, unplanned. They are triggered by words said and actions taken, as well as by those which remain unspoken and covert. A betrayer may openly deceive by taking obvious stabs at your character or status. He may tell you one thing but do something else, or pretend to care while neglecting your well-being and polluting your trust with omissions and lies. Or he may betray in a way that is subtle and hard to pinpoint, by tacitly agreeing to another's negative opinion of you, or simply by failing to be there for you when you fully anticipate that he will.

Betrayals are fueled by many forces, too—by jealousy, anger, and competition—but, surprisingly, the desire to hurt is not always one of them. Betrayers may actually wish to help you and then feel unjustly accused when you cast doubt on their credibility and motives. They may think they're being caring and protective, and that their behavior is vindicated by their admirable intentions. Do they do what they do intentionally or unwittingly? How do they live with themselves? More important, how do *you* live with *them?*

Our Cheatin' Hearts

In my private practice, I often see people reeling from the pain of betrayal. Indeed, it's hard to ignore the trust gap that slices through nearly every corner of society. Be it government, industry, education, medicine, Hollywood, sports, or the media, people and institutions we thought we could trust often turn out to be riddled with dishonesty, deception, lying, waffling, quibbling, or some other sideways bending of the truth. Though cultural historians may note that untrustworthy personal and professional relationships have been with us since time immemorial, these days they do seem more pervasive and insidious than ever.

Pollsters report that most Americans believe there is less honesty today than there was even a decade ago. Certainly, television and radio talk shows confirm that perception, with daily tales of betrayal—vows and promises broken, expectations gone haywire, relationships allowed to wither. We watch and listen as victims say that they feel alone and abandoned—adrift without an emotional compass. We watch and listen—partly with fascination, partly with empathy—because, on some level, in some way, we have all experienced their anguish. And we wonder: In a nation of adulterers, liars, swindlers, and cheaters, is being happy, rather than honorable, the New American Dream? Is there anyone we *can* count on?

Even more disturbing is that many victims have no idea how to conquer their rage, regain their dignity, and move past the trauma of broken trust. Like a paper cut, betrayal of any kind is painful, but you may tell yourself it's only a small wound, one that hurts now but will soon heal. "I'm probably making too big a deal out of this," you say, with a decided lack of conviction. And so you accept the betrayal and try hard not to let it bother you.

But it does bother you—a lot. After all, when you get cut over and over again in the same place, a small nick becomes an enduring wound that can leave a permanent scar.

THE LEGACY OF TRUST

Yet here's the paradox. Despite the dim view of what's happening in the outside world, most Americans still rank trust high on their list of virtues, invariably citing it as the most important quality they seek in a relationship—personal or professional. Indeed, to be able to trust fully is the single most important criterion for a lasting, deeply satisfying relationship. However, to trust is an active, not a passive, process. Trust can be lost, but it can also be regained.

This book is for anyone who has ever felt betrayed, abandoned, ignored, or let down by someone he trusted. No matter how badly a betrayal has wounded you, you can use what you learn here to achieve three important goals.

First, you'll be able to determine clearly what trust means to you. Once you do, you'll be better equipped to evaluate the character of the people you are dealing with—spouse or lover, family members, friends, colleagues. You'll be able to spot the warning signs that someone you trust may actually be untrustworthy, and you'll be able to anticipate emotional blackmail in all its guises.

Second, you'll be able to recognize the personal risk factors that leave you vulnerable to broken trust. Once you understand the emotional needs stemming from your past that propel you toward unstable relationships, you can shift your unrealistic expectations to more reasonable ones and protect yourself against future betrayals. Instead of feeling gullible and defenseless, you'll feel informed and powerful—capable of trusting your instincts once again.

And third, you'll learn how to manage the fallout from betrayal—when and how to confront someone who has broken your trust; when and how to let go of grudges; and when to forgive, if possible, and move on with your life. You'll shift from feeling hopeless and helpless to feeling purposeful and strong. Armed with newfound knowledge and practical, workable techniques, you can overcome the hurt, anger, and vengeful feelings that swamp you when trust is breached, and rebuild a shattered self-confidence that affects every area of your life.

Most important, rather than trusting everyone—or trusting no one—you can begin to forge and maintain healthy, nurturing relationships on every level.

SECTION I

Whom Do You Trust?

CHAPTER 1

The Trust Factor:

Four Basic Truths

For seven years, Linda and Tom were best friends as well as colleagues, having worked in the same Wall Street accounting firm since graduate school. "He was like a brother to me," Linda recalled. "We'd share everything. Whenever he had a problem in the office, I'd put aside my workload to help him figure it out." When Linda was being wooed by one of the city's top firms, it was natural for her to discuss with Tom, at length and in detail, the pros and cons of making the big move.

"Tom listened to me for hours," she continued. "While he didn't discourage me outright from accepting the offer, he didn't hesitate to point out all the reasons why I'd be happier personally—and better off professionally—if I stayed where I was."

One month later, when Linda returned from a long weekend away with her husband, her boss announced to the department that Tom had resigned. He'd been offered another job—the very position he'd discouraged Linda from accepting.

Enraged, Linda called Tom to confront him. "I thought you were my friend," she began, "but obviously my idea of friendship is different from yours. For you, it's a one-way street." Tom remained unapologetic. "Look," he told her, "I wish you had heard the news from me, but I felt I had to go through the proper work channels. I hope we can still be friends." Linda was dumbfounded. "It's not so much that you took the job," she responded coldly; "it's that you were so careless with my feelings."

Privately, she couldn't help wondering, "Why does this always happen to me? How come I didn't see that he was so selfish, he was willing to compromise our friendship to further his own career? I should have known better," she added. "Though he's not the kind of person I want for a friend, I still feel such a loss. I feel empty. How could he do this to me?"

Trust is the cornerstone of every relationship we have—an unspoken assumption about how we will behave toward, as well as be treated by, others. And because it is unspoken, we assume everyone else operates from the same reference point that we do. We expect those we trust to be faithful, loyal, and honest. In marriage, we even exchange a legal vow. With trust comes respect, personal safety, and intimacy.

And yet, at one time or another, we have all been betrayed by someone we trusted. When someone deceives us, when they hide parts of themselves or their actions from us, when they tell us only what they think we want to hear, or when they put their needs above ours, they demolish our dignity and shatter our self-esteem. Indeed, while the faces, places, and stories may change, the fallout from broken trust remains astonishingly the same: like Linda, the victims are left with a gut-wrenching emptiness and hurt. They don't feel safe any longer—emotionally, physically, spiritually, sometimes even financially.

In the wake of betrayal, many victims discover that, while they can no longer count on those who betrayed them, neither can they trust themselves. Their judgment is now faulty, their lives paralyzed. Like Linda, they ask incredulously: "Why did this happen to me? I'm a good person." Or "I'm an intelligent person, how could I let someone take advantage of me like that?" "How come I didn't realize he was a phony?" What they fail to acknowledge is that their own goodness and intelligence cannot help them anticipate, or protect them from, the malice and dishonesty of others. By learning to understand themselves and the risk factors that make them vulnerable to dishonesty, by being aware of potential betrayers and how to deal with them, they can.

The betrayal of trust often comes as a double loss. The actual betraying behavior or speech is devastating, but even more so is the breach of trust, in and of itself. Broken trust forces us, first, to acknowledge a painful reality we may have chosen to ignore, then, to make some difficult decisions. Ultimately, we may have to end a relationship that has been dear to us.

What's more, as Linda learned, a betrayal can be especially

hard to identify when roles blend. As her professional relationship with Tom grew into a friendship outside the office, the boundary between friend and colleague began to blur. Somewhere along the way, her expectations of Tom as a business colleague were eclipsed by her expectation that, as a friend, he would behave honestly with her.

THE NATURE OF TRUST

Linda is not alone. But before we can comprehend the struggle she and others face in dealing with lies and betrayals, let's first examine the elusive quality of trust, which everyone talks about but few truly understand.

Webster's gives two definitions that provide some important clues: "Trust is the assured reliance on the character, ability, strength, or truth of someone or something." The second is even more pertinent to a discussion of relationships: "One in which confidence is placed." Trust, in other words, is the glue that binds us to one another.

The psychological literature abounds with references to this most basic need. While much of what babies do and why they do it remains a mystery, research studies have shown that trust develops in the infant's earliest experiences of being cared for and protected in a constant and loving way.

Many theorists—most notably the psychiatrist John Bowlby and the sociologist Margaret Mahler—began to focus their research on these early childhood experiences. They were among the first to theorize that healthy emotional functioning is directly related to the early and consistently responsive relationship a baby has with its caregiver, usually the mother. In the late 1930s, Bowlby developed his classic theory of attachment, a specific process by which a secure, lasting, and loving bond is formed between a baby and the key people in his life. By the 1950s, Mahler spoke of the process of separation and individuation. She observed that somewhere between birth and five months of age, an infant begins to distinguish the fact that it is separate from, and not one with, its mother. Through repeated experiences of positive nurturance, a child learns to expect that its mother, father, or caregiver will be there to meet his needs and protect him: to love and care for him, to feed him when he's hungry, soothe him when he cries.

Still other theorists hypothesized about the effect of these experiences on adult attitudes and behaviors. The famed psychological theorist Erik Erikson put it best. Writing in the 1960s, he noted, "Basic trust is a state of a relationship in which a child has learned to rely on the sameness and continuity of the outside provider." Over time, Erikson explained, the child comes to feel that the world is a safe and happy place, and that he is a valued part of it. A baby who develops confidence in this consistent care will grow up to have fewer intense and chronic fears, anxieties, and less anger than one who does not. Indeed, as Bowlby had noted earlier, a secure attachment is "a principal key to the mental health of the next generation."

Consistent, reliable parenting leads to what the psychoanalyst Theresa Benedek later termed "confident expectation." With this major element in place, a child acquires a sufficient reservoir of basic trust to be able to endure unpleasant situations in the present with the expectation of gratification in the future. Children who have optimal early parenting, with consistent and regular soothing responses, will feel safe and will have the confidence to separate from their mothers, to explore, and to take risks in a world that offers pleasure and stimulation. Curiosity and wonderment will reign with respect to strangers. Whereas all children will display stranger anxiety in the first year of life, those who don't acquire basic trust may show greater degrees of anxiety with strangers than others do.

To be able to trust another person, then, is the basis of our personal security. However, because we all have different experiences growing up, we have varying definitions and expectations of trust. Indeed, as each of these theorists noted, early childhood experiences become the blueprint for how we relate to and what we expect from others. Just as the baby learns to smile and trust that his smile will be returned, the kindergartener learns to show a teacher proudly the birthday card he made for her, and the pre-teen can joke, warmly and confidently, with her best friend at school. According to Bowlby, any new person we meet—friend, teacher, spouse, boss—is incorporated into our inner attachment model. Unconsciously, we relate to him or her in much the same way we related to our initial caregivers.

ALL IN THE FAMILY

However, when the foundation for trust is weak, we grow up with a damaged sense of self and a host of unmet emotional needs. If these basic needs are not addressed—or are addressed only some of the time—we are left with a prolonged sense of longing, anticipation, and disappointment. Desperately seeking love, support, praise, and admiration, we may unwittingly enter into lopsided relationships—with lovers, family members, friends, colleagues, even our own children.

Betrayal is an abandonment and a loss. If you experience

betrayal as an adult, it may trigger feelings of longing and loss similar to those you may have had as a child. You feel totally alone, wrapped in a profound despair that your needs have been cast aside by someone you believed cared about your well-being. Under these circumstances, it can be difficult, if not impossible, to develop a secure sense of self. Since you feel unprotected and vulnerable, allowing yourself to trust someone as an adult may seem threatening, even dangerous.

What's more, those who grew up in a home in which one or both parents struggled with alcoholism, drug abuse, or other addictive behaviors that impaired their ability to respond in a reliable, trustworthy way, are particularly vulnerable to issues surrounding broken trust. Why? Because we depend on our parents to provide our moral and behavioral compass. If Mother's anger raged out of control because she drank too much and swung between periods of screaming and affection . . . if Dad promised to attend a soccer game but inevitably failed to show because he was at the racetrack, we missed out on the critical, consistent nurturing responses we needed to learn to fully trust. In fact, the research clearly suggests that if a child is raised in a family where lying, cheating, or unfaithfulness was the norm, the scars are often visible in succeeding generations.

Consider the case of Marcy, a confused and tearful attorney who came to see me because she was thinking of calling off her engagement to Rick, a fashion photographer she'd been dating for a year and a half. Marcy was reeling from the recent discovery that her adored father, a prominent banker, had been secretly having an affair with a colleague for more than ten years. He was ending his thirty-two-year marriage to Marcy's mother to marry the other woman. By all accounts, Marcy was Daddy's girl, and she was so devastated by the breakup of her parents' marriage that it wasn't long before the emotional fallout took its toll on her relationship with Rick.

"How do I know I can trust him?" she wondered aloud in my office. "Rick's a photographer. He sees beautiful women every day." When I asked whether she had any reason to doubt her fiancé's love, she admitted she had none, but that in no way lessened her anxieties or ambivalence. Though Marcy understood intellectually the correlation between the discovery of her father's infidelity and her worries over Rick's faithfulness, she was still deeply wounded by her father's act of betrayal.

If you're like Marcy, deep down you may lack self-confidence, which is another way of saying you lack a sense of self-trust—the belief that you have what it takes to accomplish what you set out to do. As a result, though successful and talented, you may find yourself in relationships that evoke all the helpless uncertainty and doubts of childhood. Such self-doubt surfaces in myriad ways. You may worry: Will I be able to make my marriage work? Am I a good enough parent? Do I have what it takes to go for that promotion at work?

Or you may grow up to be too trusting. You may seek out another person to fulfill a yearning for something you never received, despite evidence that the individual is indeed untrustworthy. Naïvely, you continue to believe, and hope, that an untrustworthy person will change—that somehow, in some way, things will be different. You convince yourself that a relationship will yield the lasting loyalty and happiness you so desperately seek; or that you alone, through your kindness, nurturing, and support, can make the relationship work. When your confidence is finally betrayed, you're dumbfounded, especially in light of all you have given. "I confided in you," you say in bewilderment. "You were my friend . . . how could you do this to me?"

What's more, if your foundation for trust is very fragile, you may never let down your guard or allow yourself to get close to anyone. Wary and suspicious, you may ultimately, albeit unconsciously, betray another. If, as a child, you experienced a traumatic loss of a parent through illness or divorce, you may protect yourself from any future loss by making sure that you are always the one to leave a close relationship rather than be the one who is left. As much as you long for an intimate relationship, you may still be too frightened and mistrustful to depend on someone else to be there for you. You may reach out, only to pull back and betray as soon as you sense yourself falling into that old trap of need. You cannot bear to experience that early emotional devastation again.

The seeds of mistrust have been sown.

BASIC TRUTHS: THE TRUST FACTOR

Trust is home to the heart; it is where we house our faith in others. But too often we trust, literally, at face value. We say to ourselves, "He looks trustworthy—professional, clean-cut, open." We assume that people are being up-front with us, and in one sense they are: they are showing us their "front," the façade they want us to see. We complete the picture.

Other times, we trust people simply because they insist we can. "Trust me on this one," they may say. But looks can be deceiving and words can be edited so that you hear what you want to hear. Oftentimes, we disregard what we see or attach our own interpretation based on what we experienced in our family of origin. In doing so, we affix our own perceptions and meanings to another's behavior. For instance, if you come from a family where lying and dishonesty were routine and automatic, you may have learned that lying is a caring behavior if it is aimed at protecting someone you love, that is, as in the little white lies you said to shield someone from pain. In an odd way, the dishonesty you may be experiencing in your current relationship feels normal. It is, after all, the way Mom and Dad related to you and to others.

Everyone's notion of trust includes an invisible but essential set of expectations that I call the Trust Factor. Family values and ideas, as well as experiences with parents and siblings, contribute to the way we interpret these expectations. There are four basic truths, or expectations, that constitute the Trust Factor. Let's take a closer look at each of them and how it affects us.

You Will Be There

When we trust someone, we expect him or her to be there for us—to support us both physically and emotionally. In a physical sense, we want him literally to be by our side, spending time, talking to us, holding us. In an emotional sense, we expect him to listen emphatically when we're beset by problems and to respond to our concerns in a way that proves he cares.

"He's never there for me" is one of the most frequent complaints heard in a therapist's office. But the problem is that "being there" means different things to different people. The disparity is especially striking in the varying definitions offered, with equal sincerity, by men and women. For most men, being there emotionally is synonymous with problem-solving. Mr. Fix-it wants to hear your problem and find a solution, now—

just the facts, ma'am. And if he's heard it once, he doesn't want to hear it a hundred times. So he closes off and moves on to the next step in his definition of "being there": solving the problem.

The following exchange between Camilla and her husband, Bruce, is a case in point. Camilla had recently started a new job with a small publishing company, but she came home after the first week overwhelmed with anxiety. The office was less organized than she had initially thought, and the scope of her job was unclear. Her new boss seemed to expect far more of her, in terms of time and output, than she felt capable of giving, and she seriously doubted her ability to handle all the responsibility suddenly thrust on her. Fearing that she had undertaken more than she could manage competently, she wanted to sit down with Bruce and vent her frustration and confusion. Bruce responded immediately, and outlined a strategy of concrete advice. Their conversation went like this:

"On Monday, Camilla, you should make an appointment with your supervisor. Tell him exactly how you feel. Remind him of what the personnel director told you at your first interview . . ."

"I don't know if I can do that," she said haltingly. "Maybe I should give it more time."

"Well, then set a deadline; say, two weeks," Bruce added, not skipping a beat. "And at the end of that time, if you're still not happy, make an appointment with your boss and outline your grievances."

"But what if . . ."

"Forget it, Camilla," Bruce shouted. "If you're going to shoot down everything I suggest, we can't talk about this."

By the time Bruce had offered what he considered three sensible solutions to Camilla's dilemma, all of which she rejected, they were quarreling and she was in tears, convinced that he didn't care about her problems and couldn't be trusted with her feelings.

Camilla, like many women, believe that being there emotionally means listening, just listening, to her as she talked about her anxieties or concerns. Often, she doesn't want to hear what she should do; she simply needs a sounding board, a person to empathize with her distress, no matter how silly or irrational it may seem. How different she would have felt if Bruce had simply said, "I can see this is very upsetting for you," and allowed her to talk rather than present her with specific solutions. She would have felt understood and safe enough to entrust him with her intimate thoughts and feelings.

Being there, for many people, also means that others will accept who you are and what you do, even if they disagree or disapprove of your opinions and actions. It means they respect you enough not to control your choices by withdrawing their support, that they will be loyal and will continue to care for you no matter what. However, passing negative judgment on a friend's actions—whether it's about the person she is marrying, the job she is taking, or the place she is moving to—is one of the most common and insidious ways that people betray a trust.

Don was shocked and hurt when his best friend, Jason, refused to return his phone calls after he told him he was asking his wife of four years, Diane, for a divorce. "Jason was best man at my wedding," Don explains, "and I know he's close to Diane. But doesn't our friendship count? I didn't pass judgment on him when he canceled his wedding a month before the ceremony." Don continues, "I thought it was a crummy thing to do, but I understood that, for him, the marriage would have been a mistake. Why is he acting so high and mighty now?"

As I said earlier, to some people the concept of trust also implies that a person will physically be there for them—visit them in the hospital or care for their children if they are ill or unable to; listen while they discuss marital woes or the loss of a job—even lend them money if they are financially strapped. "I know my brother," one man said to me recently. "No matter how much we argue—and believe me, we argue loud and often about women, politics, you name it—in a pinch, he comes through for me. We're there for each other."

In many cases, the telephone is symbolic of being there, a connection or extension cord, so to speak, to the one you trust. We expect a trusted person to prove she cares by staying in touch—on a regular basis—particularly during times of stress or crisis.

Take the case of Caitlin, who was furious at her sister Patty for not calling her. "She knows my marriage is falling apart," she told me at one session. "Patty is the only one I've spoken to about what I'm going through, how I'm going to manage with two small children if Paul and I can't work things out. And she had the nerve to tell me she couldn't talk about it anymore. I would have listened until my ear fell off if she was the one in trouble," she announced indignantly. "Now I know I can't count on her."

Patty felt defeated, frustrated, and guilty. "I listened; I tried to reason with her; I was there for her, for heaven's sake. But I have my own life to live, you know. Why does she make it seem like nothing I do is ever good enough?" Different expectations for trust set the scene for betrayal.

This Will Last

Another basic expectation of the Trust Factor is that a relationship will be ongoing and consistent, no matter what the situation. We trust in order to foster closeness and intimacy. The belief that "I can count on you time and time again" is fundamental to trust.

But often we place our trust prematurely or falsely. Perhaps we really don't know a person well enough to determine whether he merits our trust. Or perhaps we are well aware of his history of disappointment and betrayal but perpetuate a painful or unfulfilling relationship because, on some level, we are afraid to end it. We believe that the person we trust will be there, not once but always. If he disappoints us, we look beyond it to the next time, when we expect him to come through for us. Looking forward helps us move past the pain and disappointment of the moment and, more important, allows us to believe that—in time and over time—the person we trust and depend on will prove worthy. Because of our yearning for continuity, it becomes difficult to evaluate a person realistically and determine how well he matches our expectations.

Sherry is typical of people who need or want a relationship so much that they lose their perspective. Despite the admonitions of friends, Sherry refused to break up with Jed, the man she'd been living with for eight months. Jed would often tell her he had to work late on a new account—and Sherry would discover he'd really been out with friends at a bar. When she confronted him, he waffled or lied. But at other times, Jed would come home with an armful of roses, or listen sympathetically when she needed to talk about problems at work or with her family. He seemed to care . . . and during those times Sherry felt she had every reason to believe the relationship was secure.

Clearly, for Sherry and others like her, ending a bad relationship was more unbearable than living with the reality that someone she wanted to trust may have been unworthy. Ironically, her fear of abandonment kept Sherry permanently stuck in a fragile relationship that had a striking sense of impermanence.

This can happen with friends as well as lovers. Elissa and Nell met when they were both editorial assistants at a large national women's magazine, and they became fast friends. Not only did they work well together, but they had much in common: two single women with a fascination for publishing, a passion for the ballet—and a love of shopping. "I felt I had a real soulmate," recalls Elissa. "I hadn't had a friendship that deep and meaningful since college. I could tell Nell anything—and I did. We talked about personal things—our boyfriends, our ridiculous fights with our mothers. And we also shared confidences, and, I thought, helped each other strategize our careers."

Elissa didn't realize until it was too late that office friendships can be as tricky as office affairs. Nell was not as trustworthy as Elissa had thought or hoped her to be. "I see now that I confided in her way too much. I complained about my boss; we both disliked him, and I assumed that what we said to each other would go no further. But when Nell was promoted to associate editor, it hit me how wrong I was. She told our boss everything I had said about him. I can still remember how it felt to be stabbed in the back. I had lost a colleague and a friend. And now, ten years later, it still hurts when I think about it." But to be honest, she admits, she's still not sure how she could have known then what she knows now.

With the expectation "This Will Last" comes a sense of certainty and safety. This predictability—the belief that life will be okay and the hope that people will remain trustworthy—eases anxiety and offers assurance that all is right with our world.

You Will Be Honest

When we trust, we reveal our true self and let down our guard, and we expect the other person to be equally forthright, genuine, and open with us. We also expect that he will not conceal his feelings from us. If he's angry with or disappointed in us, we expect him to tell us. If he's happy and proud, we expect to hear that, too.

"You Will Be Honest" also implies that someone will talk to us before taking action that in some way affects us. Whether it's applying for a job that we, too, may be interested (as was the case with Linda and Tom); dating somebody with whom we used to be involved; or even, on a seemingly superficial level, buying the same dress or joining the same fitness club, we expect to be informed first, and not find out after the fact. What's more, if someone we trust doesn't confide in us initially, we expect that, at the very least, he'll come clean and tell us before someone else does. Certainly, he won't deny his breach of trust when we confront him about it.

Claire's relationship with Lucy, the mother of her daughter's best friend, lacked this essential element of honesty. Claire and Lucy became fast friends when their daughters entered pre-school, and they spent many hours on the park bench sharing, or so she thought, their feelings and fears about raising children. But something about the relationship bothered Claire, though she was unable to put her finger on it. Whenever she mentioned casually that her daughter was invited to a party, or had a play date with another child, she'd later find out from another mother that Lucy had called and made a date for her daughter for the same afternoon. When she signed her daughter up for a ballet class so that she'd meet other youngsters in the neighborhood, inevitably Lucy would enroll her daughter in the same class. If she told Lucy she'd arranged for a magician to perform at her daughter's birthday party, Lucy would casually announce that she'd hired the same magician *and* a clown to perform at her daughter's party, which was a month earlier. At one point, Claire learned through a mutual friend that Lucy had called her regular Saturday night baby sitter the week she was away on vacation because she was sure her friend wouldn't mind.

"I felt so uncomfortable, but I couldn't explain it," Claire told me. "Why was she doing this? It was as if we were in competition every step of the way. Whenever I started to confront her, she took great offense and made me feel like a jerk for even mentioning it. Yet, no matter what I did, she one-upped me. I started to monitor things I'd say to her and I hated myself for doing it—but for some reason, I was unable to come right out and say, 'Hey, what's going on?' I didn't like being her friend anymore. I knew she was saying things behind my back; I couldn't trust her for a minute. I repeatedly felt betrayed, but I didn't want to break it off, either. I wanted to be her friend, and I still valued aspects of our friendship. I kept hoping she wouldn't do it again." Unable to deal with the loss of a friendship, Claire felt compelled to keep alive a painful, unfulfilling relationship.

Most people give others several chances to prove themselves trustworthy. The first few times she sensed competition from Lucy, Claire rationalized her behavior. She even castigated herself for being overly sensitive and unduly suspicious. In Chapter 3, we'll talk more about why people lie and the complex, sometimes muddled nature of falsehoods. For now, it's important to understand that people do lie for many reasons but often under the guise of protection—which leads us to the next trust factor.

You Will Protect Me

Trust forms the cushion of comfort people talk about when they say, "He makes me feel safe." When we trust someone, we expect that she will not abuse personal information we shared with her. This guarantee of safety allows us to reveal our insecurities and weaknesses without fear that they will be repeated or used as weapons to shame or embarrass us.

For example, in order to explore what's troubling you and get helpful feedback, you may confide to a trusted colleague, "I'm not sure I'm good enough to make partner." Or you might say to your spouse, "I have trouble meeting new people and get very nervous when we go to a party and I don't know anyone." Or you may disclose personal information or secrets—for instance, the fact that you had an abortion when you were nineteen; that you were fired from your first job; or your fears that your teenage daughter is getting involved with a fast crowd—and expect that the information will go no further.

Holly felt the sting of betrayal keenly during an argument

with her husband, Kenny, over her ability to manage money. "We were both getting pretty nasty," Holly admits, and she's not particularly proud of some of the things she herself said. "But I couldn't believe he brought up the fact that my sister was arrested for shoplifting when she was a senior in college. He was furious at me, I know, but when he said, 'You're crazy; your whole family's crazy—look what happened to your sister,' it took the wind right out of me. I know my family has plenty of problems—but to throw that back at me in such a hurtful way . . ." Blindsided by the betrayal, Holly was speechless.

The expectation of protection also means that we believe a person we trust will not willfully hurt us or allow anyone else to hurt us. It means he will have the courage to defend our integrity when someone maligns us, rather than sit by and say nothing; that he will "do the right the thing" and, most of all, do right by us. We expect that he will not devalue us or take away what is ours, be it our possessions or, most important, our self-esteem.

If there is a breach in any one of the four expectations that make up the Trust Factor, we will feel betrayed, vulnerable, and exposed. Interestingly, the impact of broken trust varies, depending on where the breach occurs. For instance, if the breach of trust occurs in the expectation that someone we trust will be there, we will feel alone and unsupported. If it's a breach in the expectation that trust will last, our sense of well-being will be shaken. If the breach occurs in the expectation of honesty, our value system will be ruptured and, with it, our faith in the person as well as the relationship. Finally, if the breach is in the expectation of protection, our personal safety net and self-confidence will vanish.

By taking a careful look at our early childhood experiences and our parents' values, as well as understanding the way our Trust Factor operates, we may realize that some of our current relationships are not as rich and satisfying as we thought they were. Perhaps our trust is based more on our *desire* to believe in people than on having a *reason* to believe in them. Where did we go wrong? What could we do differently? That's what I'll tackle in the next chapter.

CHAPTER 2

Blind Trust:

The Five Sandtraps of Trust

Dena, a stunning woman with sun-streaked blond hair, had never before known anyone like Kevin. At twenty-six, she had just moved to Los Angeles from a small town in Northern California to take a job as a pre-kindergarten teacher. At a music industry party, she met Kevin, the handsome, highly successful owner of one of the city's hippest restaurants-cum-nightclubs. From that first night, Kevin, who was ten years her senior, seemed endearingly attentive. "I had just ended a five-year relationship with a man who swore he loved me but kept stringing me along and refused to get married," Dena recalled.

Dena wasn't used to the big city or the dating games people play, but Kevin seemed beyond that.

"He called to see me often and he went out of his way to impress my friends. I thought he cared and I was flattered by his attention," Dena said. It was a very passionate relationship, she added. "Sex was fabulous. This was really important to me, because it had been absent in my previous relationship. It made me feel good about myself, and seemed to be the one missing piece I was looking for. I could also confide in Kevin; I told him things about myself I'd never shared with anyone, and because he always listened, I thought he was really interested." Kevin, she continued, was thoughtful, too. He remembered to ask about things that had happened to her, her friends, or family. "He'd even check my refrigerator in the morning to see if I needed juice or milk—and he'd run out and get it."

Dena's friends kept telling her how lucky she was, and Dena worked hard at believing they were right, although she couldn't shake the feeling that something was amiss. There were often holes in Kevin's stories. What she didn't know then, and wouldn't find out for three months, was that Kevin had a girlfriend—and a six-month-old baby—who lived with him.

"When I discovered the truth—his so-called wife confronted me at his club one night—I was totally shocked. I felt so used," Dena recalled. "He'd promised to buy me an engagement ring! I couldn't believe he'd lie to me when I had been so up-front and honest with him. What's wrong with me? I'm not a stupid person—how could I have been such a fool?"

Dena is a victim of blind trust—and she has plenty of company. Trapped in a tangled web of misinformation, half-truths, and outright lies, many people are still alarmingly naïve when it comes to protecting themselves from the rivals, users, backstabbers, rip-off artists, and scammers—essentially, people consumed with their own self-serving needs—who betray their trust and shake their faith.

Blind trust can occur at any point in a relationship when the need to trust is so strong that people repeatedly miss the obvious signs of deception. This is the essence of blind trust: when we see only part of the picture rather than the whole . . . when we see pieces of reality but never put them together—or, if we do, never use what we've learned to adjust our behavior and feelings accordingly. For example, a boyfriend of two years repeatedly flirts with our best friend; a colleague fails to give us essential information for completing a project. Instead of understanding such behaviors for what they are, we find ways to live with what's untrue. We rationalize, minimize, or even deny someone's deceitful behavior because we want so desperately to trust. We tell ourselves, he really doesn't mean it; she's just so busy, she doesn't realize what she's doing.

Blind trust frequently operates in relationships with people you rely on. Though people often think of blind trust as applying more to the husband who "always works late at the office, and couldn't possibly be having an affair," it can also be a vital factor in relationships with nannies, housekeepers, secretaries, or even hairdressers—anyone who helps us or our family with intimate aspects of our lives. When people work in such close proximity, sharing personal experiences, roles begin to blur and we may think of them as members of the family. We've all heard the old adage "Don't take it personally; it's business." Yet inevitably, for many, it is very personal. The business aspect of a relationship is often eclipsed by the confusing ties of friendship. The misunderstandings that inevitably arise form a prime breeding ground for dashed expectations and disappointment.

Like Dena, many people think they're operating with both eyes wide open, yet fail to distinguish warning signs of dishonest behavior early enough to protect themselves from subsequent betrayals. When you look past the obvious, ignore your gut feelings, and overlook important clues, you become a victim of blind trust. You wind up seeing only what your betrayer wants you to see—and you can be wounded repeatedly.

Hindsight, of course, is often sharp. Dena now acknowledges that Kevin's untrustworthiness was blatant and that she ignored it. There was his telephone pager going off at odd hours of the day or night . . . the fact that he never gave her his home telephone number . . . the unfulfilled promises to take her to meet his mother, with whom he claimed to live . . . the countless holidays and special occasions when he swore they'd spend the whole day together, only to arrive late in the evening.

"Kevin had a plausible reason for everything," Dena says. "Even after I found out about this other woman, he kept telling me she meant nothing to him, and that I was the most important person in his life. For eight months, I took his word. I loved him. I wanted to believe him, so I kept on believing."

What forces are at work to obstruct people's ability to trust their own judgment and figure out what is really happening? As I discussed in Chapter 1, some clues can be found in the family of origin. Dena, for instance, remembers all too vividly her domineering and critical father's long absences on business, his promises, always broken, to spend more time with her. She realized later that she had been looking for a father figure, and thought she had found one in Kevin. She remembers, too, a mother who was miserable in a marriage but too passive to speak up to her super-controlling husband.

"I swore I'd never be like my mother," Dena adds. "I wasn't going to let a man treat me that way or put up with the things my mother did." Yet Dena, like others, was falling into the very pattern she tried to avoid. Despite her conscious decision to be different from her mother, she had so identified on an unconscious level with her mother's behavior that she replicated it in her relationship with Kevin. People often repeat the past in an attempt to resolve old, painful feelings of disappointment and abandonment and to get the love and attention they feel they missed out on. Despite good intentions, early, unconscious identifications and learned family behaviors are often so strong that they are difficult to avoid or overcome.

Another reason people succumb to blind trust is an obvious one: they're simply unable to detect when a person isn't telling the truth. You may assume that if someone looks trustworthy and sounds trustworthy, he can be trusted. You base your trust on your own beliefs and perceptions rather than on reality. Part of this stems from the effect that appearance has in determining what we think of the people we choose to admire. Witness how horrified we are when the sports figures or film and television celebrities we idolize fail to live up to their images. On some level, we feel betrayed by their actions, because they don't look like people who would do the things they've allegedly done. We're deceived by their images—on the silver screen or the playing field.

Even in our personal interactions, we continue to rely on surface qualities—facial expressions, gestures, changes in voice —oblivious that these qualities often yield highly inaccurate readings. In fact, in the judicial community it is well known that what a defendant wears, as well as his physical presence—his race, his weight, even the way he wears his hair—plays a critical role in the jury's deliberations and can mean the difference between a guilty or not guilty verdict.

Olivia considered herself a street-smart New Yorker, yet she was easily misled by personal appearance. "You can't pull the wool over my eyes," she thought. Yet while vacationing at a posh resort in Jamaica, Olivia and her friend met a nice-looking man at dinner who invited them to take a drive around the island. Ultimately, this seemingly nice man stalked them for the rest of night, until they were forced to call the police. Why did she do something when common sense would dictate otherwise?

"To tell you the truth," she told me ruefully, "he looked perfectly respectable. Nicely dressed in khakis and a V-necked sweater, he looked every inch the Midwestern businessman he professed to be."

Clearly, people who are hurt, deceived, or betrayed never want to be fooled again, by the same person or by someone new. Yet on some level, all wounded individuals are in the dark. They don't know how they got into trouble in the first place, and they don't know what to look for to prevent it from happening again. What they often fail to understand is that trust is a process; it takes time to make it and it takes time to break it. Not that we should be suspicious of every person who walks into our life. But real trust must develop over time, based on a person's behavior and consistent responses. There is no such thing as trust at first sight.

At the center of blind trust is its importance in buttressing our self-esteem as well as our sense of right and order in our lives. After all, to be able to trust is a virtue. Trusting feels good and honorable, whereas being suspicious and skeptical seems petty and superficial. Second, trusting another, regardless of whether he merits it, is one way to manage an array of negative feelings—including anger, disappointment, anxiety, uncertainty, and guilt—that emerge when we're confronted with another's hurtful behaviors. Blind spots allow us to deny the obvious or the painful: Unconsciously, we may avoid seeing a spouse's infidelity or a sister's attempts to cheat us out of an inheritance in order to postpone the inevitable confrontation with the betrayer—and with the truth. We suspend critical judgment and ignore contradictory information, because uncovering that truth is more traumatic than believing the lie.

But the main reason people trust blindly is that they cling to five beliefs that prevent them from seeing reality. While there are elements of truth in each of these beliefs, when you cleave to them to the exclusion of all other evidence, you lose your perspective and stumble along, easily duped or taken advantage of by the betrayers that cross your path. You may even remain in relationships that are emotionally and physically dangerous, because you see no way out or, worse, no reason to exit.

These beliefs, taken to the extreme, become sandtraps, snaring you in potentially hurtful relationships. Recognizing the following sandtraps that may be affecting your actions is the first step in freeing yourself from unhappy, untrustworthy relationships.

TRUST SANDTRAP #1:
YOU MUST GIVE SOMEONE
THE BENEFIT OF THE DOUBT

Our need to trust is powerful. That's because trust is a protective shield that keeps out the hurt and the loneliness so that we continue to feel valued, worthy, and loved. When we trust, we cast aside our doubts, and have faith that our relationships are secure and fulfilling, our decisions sound, our futures bright.

However, some people's need to trust is so strong that they repeatedly rationalize, minimize, negate, or deny another person's hurtful words or actions, ignore their intuition, and push acts of deceit out of their field of vision.

You're stuck in this sandtrap if you repeatedly tell yourself, "It's not what I think it is," or "I'm being unreasonable; it's not nice to attribute ulterior or malicious motives to others." You're also trusting blindly if you believe a betrayer when she denies or excuses her actions, insisting, "I didn't say that . . . "That's not what I meant" . . . "It's not what you think it is." In this case, she is misleading you with half-truths, giving you just enough to work with and believe so that you misinterpret what she really means and, instead, turn it into what you want it to be.

That's what happened to Rochelle, a purchasing agent for an import-export company. "What should I do now?" she said in a plaintive voice as she walked into my office. She hadn't seen Roy, the man she met at a friend's party, in three months.

"We had a wonderful time that night and I fell head over heels for him," Rochelle told me. "He's everything I want in a man, and we spent two great weekends together. I'd let it go if he didn't give me every indication that he still wants to see me."

Roy calls Rochelle every night, and they talk for at least half an hour. He makes dates for the weekend; then, inevitably, cancels at the last minute with effusive apologies and reassurances of his continuing love. Rochelle can't stop thinking about him or bring herself to end the relationship, and she continues to assume that Roy's intentions are good, despite contrary indication. He has given her just enough to go on, so she won't let go of the relationship while he holds his options open.

What keeps people like Rochelle stuck in Sandtrap #1 is the unspoken concern: "What's wrong with me? Why am I so suspicious?" The real question she should be asking herself is: "How many times do I accept excuses before I feel compelled to confront the truth?" If you give someone the benefit of the doubt too often, because you feel guilty and think you should believe him, you wind up doubting yourself and compromising your self-esteem. You should not always dismiss what happens as a misunderstanding; rather, you must confront situations, question them carefully, and clarify the confusion.

TRUST SANDTRAP #2:
YOU SHOULD GIVE SOMEONE A
CHANCE TO PROVE HE'S TRUSTWORTHY

As members of society, we place a high premium on honesty and integrity. Most of us want to be truthful, to know that others can trust us, and to believe that we can trust them. What's more, if someone admits he has breached our trust, we want to think we're big enough to forgive him and give him another shot. It makes us seem like the good guy, and we automatically feel better about ourselves.

Fran was tired of listening to her husband's litany of excuses for never managing to make it home before nine-thirty —often later—every night, or remember to call and tell her where he was. "Shawn works for a high-powered real estate firm in the city," Fran explained. "I know the pressure to make deals and drum up new business is intense—the pace is much faster than his first job. But does that mean late dinners at fancy restaurants every night? I never see him during the week anymore, and half the time I'm worried sick that he's wrapped around a telephone pole somewhere." Though Shawn reassured her that he always went out with people from work, he'd grown increasingly distant over the past few months, and she couldn't help wondering whether he was having an affair. Though she hated herself for it, Fran grew suspicious and began to check her husband's briefcase and jacket pockets.

"I started to catch him in little lies. He'd tell me he never went to a particular restaurant and then I'd find a napkin or credit card receipt that proved he had." Each time she confronted him, Shawn would get defensive, tell her he was sorry, he'd gotten confused, and then swear he'd remember to call next time he'd be late. "Before I knew it, I'd wind up apologizing to him," Fran admitted. The night Fran was sick with bronchitis, and Shawn again failed to call, she told him he either had to go with her for marriage counseling, or she would file for divorce.

You, too, may be stuck in this second sandtrap if you consistently find that the times you need another person the most are when you can depend on him the least. What's more, in spite of frequent let-downs, you continue to reassure yourself by saying, "I'm sure it won't happen again," or "His intentions are good; I'll give him another chance."

At the crux of Sandtrap #2 is this nagging doubt: "If I don't give him a second chance, am I being unforgiving and unaccepting?" However, the question you should be asking is: "Are his words true to his actions?" Remember, in a healthy relationship you can't simply accept verbal reassurance that whatever happened to betray your trust won't happen again. For some people, it's easy to say they're sorry— and nothing more. You must see changed behaviors and actions that demonstrate trustworthiness.

Trust Sandtrap #3:
You Should Accept
the Good with the Bad

Most of us believe that people are basically good, and because we do, we have considerable resiliency when it comes to accepting obviously hurtful behavior. However, when we start to focus on such actions and label them for what they really are, many of us, paradoxically, wind up feeling guilty about being angry or being judgmental. We think, "I'm being petty"; "I'm making a mountain out of a molehill"; "After all, nobody's perfect." We feel we are being too demanding and unreasonable: "What's wrong with me? Why can't I be more tolerant and understanding?" In addition, we frequently absorb blame for another's behavior and assume the other person is acting in a certain way because *we* are doing something wrong.

For example, Maxine's husband, Lenny, is an incorrigible flirt. Whenever they go to a party, he spends most of the evening laughing with and ogling every other woman in the room, leaving Maxine feeling ignored and unimportant. When she tries to talk to him about it, he scoffs, "You're being ridiculous. I'm just having fun. Lighten up."

With their first child due in a few months, Maxine tried to convince herself that she was making too big a deal about the whole matter. "After all, that's the way guys are," she added. "Besides, I was seven months pregnant, looked like a beached whale, and didn't have a whole lot of energy. I'm sure my appearance and attitude had a lot to do with his actions. If I change, he'll change." But even when she cut her hair the way he wanted her to, she found he still wasn't affectionate with her. What's more, nothing she tried, including adopting a lighthearted attitude, would please him.

Therein lies the crux of this sandtrap. While it may feel good to bring out the best in another, and though it may even give you the sense that you have a measure of control over the situation, you really don't. Continuing to forgive hurtful actions is unhealthy. You need to set limits and to expect specific changes in the behavior of someone you trust. Maxine set limits by telling Lenny, "I'm really upset; we need to talk to somebody." In the safety of my office, she shared with him how she felt and specifically what she needed to feel supported and loved—more attention, more hugs, and fewer derogatory comments about her appearance, even in jest. At the same time, Lenny was able to voice his fears about having a baby. Once he discussed them with Maxine, he no longer had to act them out by flirting with everyone in a skirt.

TRUST SANDTRAP #4:
I'M TRUSTWORTHY;
YOU WILL BE, TOO

We often expect people to be just like us and abide by our value system. If we always behave with integrity and try to protect and look out for others, we assume others will do the same for us. Why wouldn't someone else? However, making such a Pollyanna-like assumption can be another fruitless attempt to make your world safe.

Julie, an office worker in Minneapolis, was shocked to learn that a comment she had made over lunch with a colleague had found its way to their supervisor—who subsequently excluded her from an important project. Julie was incredulous. "I would *never* tell the boss something a colleague tells me in confidence; I thought we were friends—I can't believe she did that!"

Like Julie, you may be stuck in this sandtrap if you find yourself discounting obvious signs that a colleague is vying for your position; that a business proposition that promises to be "too good to be true" probably is; or that an apparently nurturing, empathic lover has no intention whatsoever of making a lifetime commitment. The crux of this sandtrap is that you can never merely assume someone will behave in a trustworthy manner. What's more, what may seem like a breach of trust to one person may be perfectly acceptable to another. To protect yourself from manipulative behavior, let down your guard only when you see real demonstrations of trustful behavior; when you find that promises are kept and your secrets safeguarded.

Trust Sandtrap #5:
We Share the Most Intimate
Details of Our Lives,
so I Know I Can Trust You

When people share their most personal thoughts and feelings with each other, they may falsely believe that the very revelations, in and of themselves, render the relationship trustworthy. When they expose their vulnerabilities, weaknesses, shameful or embarrassing past experiences, they feel they are being genuine and real. People will often say, "I know I can trust him, because I can really be myself with him."

Ivy had been dating Nick for a year and a half when she found him in bed with another woman. "I can't believe he did this to me," she said tearfully when she came to see me. Ivy had heard about Nick's reputation as a ladies' man even before they started dating, but she claimed, "I thought he'd changed; he really seemed to want to settle down. We were so close, and I thought I knew him so well." Nick, she reported, had told her about his mother's battle with alcoholism, and how lonely he had been growing up, never knowing from one day to the next if she'd be sober or drunk when he came home from school. "There were tears in his eyes when he told me," Ivy added. "I just melted. He was such a tough, macho kind of guy on the outside, and here he was, revealing these incredibly personal stories. He even told me I was the first person he could really be himself with. The fact that I could break through that tough shell in a way no other woman ever could made me feel special, that the relationship was unique. How could I not trust a man who was that open and honest?"

That's precisely the point: you shouldn't. Like Ivy, you've fallen into Sandtrap #5 if you believe that self-disclosure constitutes a basis for trust. People share personal details and information for many different reasons: to foster closeness, even to control another's actions.

An exchange of intimacies cannot stand on its own. It's not what is said to another, but what a person does with what he's told that marks the difference between a sound trusting relationship and one that is potentially disappointing or hurtful. To extricate yourself from Sandtrap #5, you must ask: Is the sharing balanced? Do his actions merit my trust?

As I've discussed, the dynamics stemming from your family of origin, the tendency to judge people at face value, coupled with the trust sandtraps in which many people get stuck, make you vulnerable to blind trust. But while trusting blindly is quite common, it is also foolish—and dangerous. By continuing to ignore the reality that someone can't be trusted, you may become so dependent on him that when his behavior abruptly changes—or when he seeks to end the relationship entirely—you will be bereft.

CHAPTER 3

"*I Did It Because*":

Why Betrayers Betray

Who are these people who break a trust and threaten a cherished relationship with deceit and lies? Why do they act in seemingly inexplicable ways? How can they live with themselves—and, more important, how can you continue to live with them? Before I can answer these questions, we have to understand the nature of betrayal in the first place.

Webster's tells us that to betray means to lead astray; to fail or desert in time of need; to reveal unintentionally; to disclose a confidence. The most common, most obvious form of betrayal is lying, a word that, once again, means different things to different people. According to Sissela Bok, a professor of ethics at Brandeis University and author of the classic book *Lying: Moral Choice in Public and Private Life,* lying is "any intentionally deceptive message which is stated." Paul Ekman, a psychiatrist at the University of California, Los Angeles, and author of *Telling Lies,* notes that out-and-out fabrication—when someone knows he is lying and goes right ahead and does it anyway—is but a small part of lying. There are, he adds, lies of omission, lies of concealment, and half-truths—leaving out information that another would normally expect to be there. What's more, he notes, lying isn't limited to words or misleading statements. People lie through their behavior, too—their actions, gestures, silences that tacitly support a lie—as well as by presenting false information as if it were true, or by acknowledging an emotion but misidentifying what caused it.

Paradoxically, while we all insist on truthfulness and extoll honesty, we all lie. Even a casual glance at the daily newspaper proves that, as a society, we've come to accept, even expect, duplicity and deception as part of our social fabric. After all, political leaders do it; football and baseball heroes do it; Madison Avenue advertising executives do it; the stars of stage and screen do it; the heads of major corporations and savings and loan institutions do it; journalists in the quest of headline-making stories do it; even scientists at prestigious research laboratories do it.

Indeed, as we head toward a new millennium, we get an almost pervasive sense that people feel they must do what is necessary and expedient to succeed—honesty be damned. Whether it's a big lie on a grand scale or petty gossip spread around the water cooler at work or in the neighborhood playground, lying, betrayal, and lack of trust are as much a part of the American way as truth and justice. In fact, there are as many different types of lies as there are liars.

At one end of the spectrum is the little white lie—the well-intentioned nicety we say to protect someone's feelings. "You look great," we tell a friend who has actually gained far too much weight since we last saw her. "That was delicious, but I'm much too full for seconds," we say with forced gusto to a relative whose culinary creations we are barely able to swallow. In fact, life would be unbearable if we never lied. When we ask the receptionist at the front desk, "How are you?" we don't want to hear a litany of complaints about her husband, her kids, her mother-in-law, and the sick cat that threw up on the bed last night. We want her to say, "Just fine, thanks."

Sometimes people lie to avoid a hassle, petty arguments, or to escape a burdensome social experience: "I'm so sorry I can't make the party on Saturday, but we have long-standing plans with my husband's business partner." They may even lie to show off, to enhance their prestige and make themselves look better or more important: "I was a cheerleader in high school and vice president of the student council."

There is another motivation for lying and betrayal that often results in a Catch-22. Many people feel they are forced to lie to protect themselves from the anger, disappointment, jealousy, and the potentially controlling behavior that can arise when the persons with whom they're involved learn something about them which they may dislike or disapprove.

For example, Jody and Glenn vividly remembered the pain and longing they had each suffered as a result of their respective parents' divorces when they were children. As a result, Jody, in particular, tried desperately to be as honest and forthright with her new husband as she could be. "One of the reasons my parents' marriage broke up is that my mother had had a string of affairs—mostly with married men—and I swore I would never be like her," Jody explained when she and Glenn first came for treatment. "So I bared my soul to Glenn. I told him that I had been involved with a married man before I had met him, and I'd broken it off because I realized how destructive that relationship could be."

But Jody's revelations boomeranged. As they grew closer, Glenn became increasingly anxious and suspicious about Jody's past and what it might mean for their future together. "He interrogated me about old boyfriends and things I'd done years ago. It was an assault on my character," she remembered. "Then he'd add: 'How do I know you won't do what your mother did?' "

Despite reassurances, nothing Jody said or did could assuage Glenn's conviction that she would betray him. "I was so worn down by this barrage of antagonistic questioning that before I realized what I was doing, I found myself lying, actually telling him things that weren't true, because I couldn't stand the inquisition." In time, Jody got caught in the web of lies she had constructed to protect herself from Glenn's jealousy. "I couldn't remember every little thing I told him. So every once in a while, he'd catch me in a little lie. Then he'd blow up and berate me, and before long, he was into a full-blown attack all over again, declaring, 'How can I ever trust you when you lie?' But he's the one who sets me up all the time."

By the time they came to see me, Glenn was convinced that he could never trust Jody. It took a long time for him to realize that, by being so suspicious and controlling, he was perpetuating the very behavior of which he was most fearful. In fact, his obsessive jealousy of what he perceived as Jody's betrayal became a self-fulfilling prophecy and was driving her away. In session, Glenn recognized that Jody was being genuine and honest with him, and because of this, he was in time able to build the foundation he needed to trust.

Jay, an insurance salesman, was in a similar predicament. Jay had had a two-month affair with Andrea, a woman he met at the office, but he'd ended it six months before, and he and his wife came for counseling. Now, their marriage seems back on track, except for Helene's constant vigilance and fear that he would again be unfaithful. Last month, Jay went to visit his father after work and, on the bus, bumped into his former lover. They had a pleasant, innocuous conversation—but Jay was wracked with guilt.

"A part of me wants to tell my wife that I ran into Andrea; I'd feel I was lying if I didn't. But we're getting along so well now, I don't want to screw anything up." The problem, he said, is that Helene is so jealous and so suspicious—she asks more questions than an FBI investigator—that Jay is concerned that his merely mentioning the other woman's name will open up wounds he's tried hard to heal. "It sounds terrible, but it's easier to lie," he said. "I'm not happy about it, but I don't know what else to do."

When treating people like Jay, I outline their options, which many times they are unable to see clearly or prioritize. I told him that if he continued to leave things out, he would always feel that he was doing something wrong. "You must learn to deal directly with Helene about issues large and small. Then you can begin to help her put the incident into perspective." Often the fact that you are being honest and trusting someone to understand goes a long way to healing wounds inflicted on her self-esteem.

WHEN NEEDS COLLIDE

The process of bending the truth starts young. We instruct our children, "Tell Grandma I'm in the shower," when your mother-in-law, whom you don't want to talk to, is on the phone. In fact, children watch parents lie all the time. When the parents want to avoid a family holiday dinner, suddenly Mommy has a cold. Or consider the busy mother who doesn't want to yield to yet another request to play a video game at the mall: "No, Michael, Mommy doesn't have any money right now."

Such seemingly small social fibs to avoid conflict and complications become habits, ones we don't notice we've fallen into. Yet, in time or on a larger scale, such behavior fosters a cynical view that it's acceptable to manipulate and control another person for short-term gain or personal advantage. The result is a violation of trust, the severing of bonds that give strength to personal relationships, to our community, and to our society as a whole.

While we tend to automatically label those who break a trust as malicious, many times, as you'll note in the following story, they may view the situation from an entirely different perspective and behave accordingly.

Meredith, director of corporate development for a prestigious investment bank, and Beverly, who now holds a similar spot at another firm, became fast friends when they were fresh-out-of-college associates, and remained best friends, although they were competitive in their work, over the next ten years as they each moved up the corporate ladder. But when

Meredith was home on maternity leave with her first child, the women's friendship was put to a test—one that, ultimately, it could not survive.

Six weeks into her leave, Meredith received a call from Harriet, her boss, who told her she was considering asking Beverly to join the management staff. "She said she wanted to hire her, though she was very vague and wouldn't tell me for what position," Meredith recalled, "and she asked me what I thought. Well, I went into panic mode. Semihysterical from lack of sleep and trying to deal with a colicky baby, feeling my hormones rampaging, I was in no condition to think calmly. I mumbled something and got off the phone, but continued to stew about it for days."

Meredith became even more agitated a week later, when Beverly called to report on the "fabulous" lunch she had just had with Harriet, and how excited she was at the prospect of being able to work with Meredith again. Although Harriet had, in subsequent phone calls, reassured Meredith that she had nothing to worry about—in fact, even hinted that a big promotion would soon come her way—Meredith's anxieties and uncertainty about what she should do increased.

"I knew Beverly was miserable where she was, and I wanted to be a loving and supportive friend. But I was terribly conflicted and not all that sure I wanted to work in the same company with my best friend," Meredith explained frankly. "We're in senior positions now, and that presents a very different situation from when we were juniors just starting out. I told Bev I was seriously afraid our friendship would be jeopardized."

Beverly was flabbergasted and could not understand Meredith's point of view. As the weeks passed, and Harriet still made no hiring decisions, the tension between the two women heightened. In the end, Meredith did receive a promotion, and Harriet ultimately decided not to hire Beverly after all. But the friendship between Meredith and Beverly was damaged beyond repair.

Even now, two and a half years later, Beverly is still reeling with hurt and anger at what, to her, was an obvious attempt by a trusted friend to sabotage her career and her happiness. "She recently told a colleague of mine that she will never understand why or how I could betray her like that," Meredith reports sadly, "and there are many days when I can't help wondering if that's exactly what I did do. If I hadn't been so insecure, so desperate to protect my own turf, wouldn't I have been more generous?"

Meredith continues to struggle with conflicting feelings. "I suppose I should have felt relieved and excited that my worst fears didn't materialize," Meredith sighs, "but I didn't feel that way, not at all. I lost a friendship that had meant a great deal to me. I felt lousy—and guilty. Bev thinks I stabbed her in the back, that I was somehow instrumental in my boss's decision not to hire her—in fact, that I probably used the whole affair to leverage a promotion for myself. But that's not what I wanted or what I did. In my wildest imagination, I never expected all this to happen. Of course, I'll never convince her of that."

The experience has changed her in another way, too. "I lost a dear friend, and I will always feel that hole in my life. But I will never again allow work friends to become personal friends," she vows. "The potential for conflict is always there. I'm more guarded now. I shut down and edit out many of my feelings and thoughts with certain people. I don't want to be like that, but what choice do I have?"

Meredith's dilemma, and Beverly's very different perception of it, is typical of the confusion and misunderstanding surrounding many cases of broken trust. Betrayal, like beauty, is often in the eyes of the beholder: you think someone is acting against you when he or she is simply acting for himself, with no thought of you whatsoever. In fact, time and again, what appear to be obvious and deliberately hurtful actions to one individual mean something entirely different to another. What one person may deem a necessary disclosure, a healthy venting of angry feelings, or a reasonable attempt to protect what is rightfully hers, another will see as inappropriate, obnoxious, hostile, even violating. Meredith should have written her friend a letter, explaining how much she valued their friendship and that she never meant for her to feel betrayed. She should have told the truth: she was caught up in her own needs and is sorry her friend was hurt as a result.

Another reason trust issues are so complicated and puzzling is that truth and honesty are often relative. Though as a society we like to think otherwise, people differ markedly in their capacity for tolerating deception and what, in their mind, constitutes acceptable, honest, and ethical behavior. One person may engage in little social, face-saving lies or deceptions, think nothing of taking home pens and pencils from work for her children, or of making the occasional personal call from the office phone. In fact, she may assume everyone else does, too. Another person, however, may be horrified by such actions, and would never think of saying or doing anything that is not scrupulously honest. Such a person may also have a fierce sense of righteousness and justice; she's convinced that if someone has lied once, he'll lie again. Someone else is more tolerant, able to excuse, even empathize, with the betrayer. This person can more easily allow a disappointment or breach of trust to roll off her back.

Why the discrepancy? Just as our capacity to trust is forged early on, so too is our perception of, and tolerance for, betrayal. If our parents acted dishonestly, if they told us one thing but did another, if we knew they engaged in extramarital affairs, or if they repeatedly denied our own perception of what was happening around us, we may well have a high tolerance for what others consider dishonest, unethical, or false. On the other hand, if in general we had a loving, nurturing family experience, where people were mutually supportive, we will not only expect people to be there for us, but we will most likely choose to associate only with those who are reliable, dependable, and trustworthy.

WHY THEY DO IT

Nevertheless, there are compelling reasons that people fail us. Many betrayals are clearcut: they're motivated by greed, revenge, fear of another's anger, or fear of what one may personally lose. Betrayals are about trying to gain, trying to get even, or trying to protect oneself from another.

Betrayals may also be motivated by the need to avoid or escape blame or disapproval or to cover up a mistake. We see this often in the passive-aggressive type of lie or half-truth. "Okay, you're right. I should have told you I didn't get around to making the airline reservations," Annie's husband, Russell, snapped, "but I knew you wouldn't understand. You'd be furious and scream at me."

The majority of betrayals, however, are decidedly more subtle—and therein lies the dilemma for those who are easily tripped up by their desire and need to trust. At what point does a misunderstanding, a lack of awareness, or a simple passing on of information cross the invisible boundary and become an outright betrayal of confidence and breach of trust? The distinction is often small and a matter of degree. For instance, sometimes people betray under the guise of protection. "I did this for you," they claim; "I didn't want you to be hurt." Though this may sound like a suitable justification, the truth is that many times people don't particularly want our protection; they'd rather know the cold hard truth, thank you very much, than hear a lie, a fib, or a fudged truth, however well-intended.

Basically, there are three main categories of betrayals: *unaware betrayals; couldn't-help-it betrayals;* and, finally, *deliberate betrayals.* To protect ourselves from repeated disappointments, we must be able to distinguish between them.

Unaware Betrayals

"I didn't do anything to you." "What are you talking about?" "Do what? I was only trying to help."

Betrayal is determined by the person who feels it. In this type of betrayal, a person is honestly unaware that she has failed you. Many times, she has betrayed you to gain some sort of advantage for herself. Still, if you ask such a betrayer, "How could you do this to me?" she will most likely say, with genuine surprise, "Do what?" Motivated purely by her self-interest, oblivious of your feelings or position, she does not realize she has crossed the boundaries of trust. Of course, some people do not see this as a betrayal at all. However, when the shoe is on the other foot, they also would feel betrayed if a person they trusted failed to inform them of such matters.

What's more, such a person does not comprehend the impact of her behavior or how a relationship may blow up in her face as a result of it. Nonetheless, we feel violated. Why? Because this type of betrayal springs from your Trust Factor gone awry (see Chapter 1). Having certain expectations for trust, you assume a person will behave in a certain way. When she doesn't, or when you misconstrue her motives, you feel betrayed.

Many times, unaware betrayals are paternalistic in nature— that is, people betray under the guise of caring and trying to help, or to spare another pain, trouble, or unpleasant news. They think they are looking out for us and have our best interests at heart. In reality, such betrayals are often naïvely intrusive and ultimately controlling.

A common example of this type of betrayal is the person who decides to tell you that your husband is having an affair, your son is smoking pot, or your daughter is hanging out with an unsavory crowd. He feels it is his place to inform you so that you can take what he deems necessary action. He is staggered that you feel violated by his revelation and betrayed by his act of telling.

Arlene's experience with her sister is a typical example of a betrayal motivated by paternalistic feelings. When Arlene learned that her son Brett had attention deficit disorder, she talked at length about her feelings with her sister, Mona. "On one hand, I was very upset," Arlene recalls, "but I was also somewhat relieved. Brett's behavioral and academic problems, all those years of pain and unhappiness, suddenly made sense. At last, we felt we were on the right track, that something was finally being done to help Brett and us." Mona knew how traumatic the whole process had been for her sister, which is why Arlene was shocked when she walked into her sister's home on Christmas Day and was accosted by a woman, whom she barely knew, sympathizing with her son's problems and relating some of the same frustrations she was having with her own son.

"Okay, so she was my sister's friend and I suppose, from her perspective, she was trying to help. I probably wouldn't have minded if Mona had asked me first. What hurts is that she didn't think for a second about revealing a personal confidence. She should have known." Arlene believes there's no point in even discussing with Mona how betrayed she feels. "She'd look at me as if I had two heads. She's always been like this. I'll be astonished by the things she does, the flagrant breaches of a confidence, but she doesn't have a clue. She thinks she's looking out for me."

Mona has no idea that her sister feels this way. That's why Arlene must acknowledge that, while her sister's motivation may have been well-intended, the result was a painful breach of trust. She needs to set limits by saying, "In the future, I'd rather that you not bring this matter up with other people. It makes me feel uncomfortable."

Couldn't-Help-It Betrayals

"I never meant for this to happen." "It's not what I thought would happen."

These betrayers know that, on some level, they are doing something others will find objectionable, but they feel compelled to do it, anyway. Warren was an unwitting betrayer when, following the death of his elderly mother, he accepted for himself the fee generally accorded the executor of an estate. "My younger brother Adam blew his stack," Warren reported with genuine confusion. "Mother had divided her assets evenly between us, but since I lived nearby, it made sense for me to administer the will. The paperwork is mindboggling, and it took a lot of time, so I simply assumed that I was entitled to the executor's fee. Everyone knows that. But Adam didn't see it that way at all. He actually called me a greedy traitor."

Warren is only one type of couldn't-help-it betrayer. Whereas he knew his brother might misunderstand and object to his collecting a fee, he was genuinely shocked at the depth of anger his action elicited and puzzled to discover that his actions had been construed as anything less than scrupulous. Meredith, the woman we met earlier in this chapter, also knew what she was doing. Still, she too falls into the category of couldn't-help-it betrayer. While she was no doubt trying to gain an advantage, she did not intend to hurt Beverly. So caught up in her own needs, so threatened by what she perceived as a possibly lost position, she justified her actions by convincing herself that there was no other way to handle the situation.

Like betrayers who are wholly aware of their actions, couldn't-help-it betrayers betray in order to protect their turf. They use their resources and power to ensure their success—perhaps at the expense of yours—though there is no true intent on their part to hurt you. This betrayer knows what he is doing—and may not like himself for it—but believes his action is necessary to protect himself. Tom, the man we met in the beginning of Chapter 1, is also a couldn't-help-it betrayer. As he said about Linda, the woman he deceived when he competed for the job she wanted, "After I talked her out of it, I realized how good the position sounded. But I was too embarrassed and ashamed to tell Linda what I had done."

Deliberate Betrayals

"You made me do it." "I don't care; I did what I had to do."

These are the deliberate, insidious betrayals, born of revenge and retaliation and inflicted by a person who believes himself to be so entitled and/or wronged that he feels justified in acting the way he does. His need to repair his emotional damage is so strong that he does whatever he must to get his needs met. He may go to great lengths to conceal his betraying behavior. On the other hand, he may actually flaunt his hurtful actions, so intent is he on making you pay the price for his pain. The point to remember about deliberate betrayals is that the people who cause them often feel wronged and may view you as responsible in some way. That may or may not be true; nevertheless, it is their belief, and it fuels their betraying behavior. You may never be able to convince them that they are wrong. This is their truth, and they believe their actions are valid.

Aware betrayals often occur in the gray area where business and personal relationships overlap. It is one of the prime breeding grounds for such actions and often the most difficult trust terrain to navigate. Aware betrayals are especially common when the nature of the business fosters a kind of intimacy that many people misconstrue as a personal closeness—real estate, travel planning, beauty services, interior design, and architectural planning, to name a few.

When Gina, a travel agent, worked for a large tour company, her boss asked her to work with one of the firm's major clients. Though she became good friends with the client's wife, and would often socialize with them as a couple, she found the husband domineering and obnoxious. Nevertheless, she always hid her feelings behind a veneer of corporate politeness and efficiency.

However, when Gina quit her job to form her own agency, she decided not to inform this particular couple of her plans, though she did tell other people with whom she had previously worked. She was distressed to pick up the phone one day and hear a tirade of abuse coming from her former client's wife.

"She had learned from someone else that I had left and she was hurt and furious that I had never called her. She actually told me I had betrayed her," Gina says. "And I suppose in a way I did. But I had to think of myself. I couldn't stand working with her husband any longer, and now I didn't have to."

Aware betrayals may also occur when one person is hurt upon discovering another's aware betrayal—for example, the wife who learns of her husband's infidelity and has an affair with a co-worker, either to get even or to make sure he doesn't hurt her again.

The behavior of Molly, who works in the clothing business, exemplifies aware betrayal. Molly has been married for six years to Ted, a controlling, inattentive textile manufacturer with whom she had eloped to escape living with her cold and domineering parents. But Ted turned out to be just as insensitive as they were, and over the years, Molly became increasingly depressed.

"This is a man who is so wrapped up in his business that he didn't even manage to make it to the hospital when I gave birth to our daughter," Molly explained. Little wonder that she sought solace in Evan, her boss, who was as acknowledging and admiring of her abilities as Ted was demeaning. In time, she even became very close with Evan's wife, Penny; the women would often take their children to Gymboree classes and then spend the rest of the day together.

But during the week that Penny was out of town visiting her mother, Evan and Molly began an affair. Most people would be shocked to hear that a woman like Molly could sleep with the husband of one of her closest friends. But the truth is, actions like Molly's take place all the time. How does she live with herself? How can she continue to be friends with Penny, knowing that she's sleeping with her husband?

"I'm sickened with guilt," Molly admits haltingly. "And yet I can't stop myself. The rest of my life is so barren, so empty. And I know that Evan is as unhappy in his marriage as I am in mine. He gives me something I don't think I could survive without," she adds to justify her betrayal.

Despite her remorse, Molly feels powerless to change. In such cases, the act of betrayal is the way that people like Molly protect themselves from the pain they are experiencing in their present relationship, pain that is reminiscent of the feelings of abandonment they felt in childhood.

CROSSING THE LINE

As I have said, the first step in moving beyond betrayal is to understand why the people we trust have let us down. In this first section, I discussed the roots of trust and the expectations we have for the way other people will treat us. We also explored the subtle but powerful family dynamics that propel us into vulnerable relationships of all kinds, as well as the nature of betrayal and the reasons that motivate people to betray us.

Needless to say, when you've been run over by someone's betraying behavior, it will hardly matter to you why he did it. You're hurt and upset, and that's all you care about. However, when it comes to repairing the damage, the motivation for betrayal becomes very relevant. These motivations may help you determine whether to make amends, or whether it's time to consider permanently ending the relationship.

I'll examine the choices you have in later chapters. Now it's time to take a closer look at the people who have crossed the line between trust and betrayal. In this next section, I profile the Rival, the Admirer, and the User, the three main types of betrayers everyone meets at some point in her life. I'll explain how you can recognize them before you succumb to their acts of deceit, as well as how to pinpoint the specific risk factors that render you especially vulnerable to each type of betrayer.

HIS CHEATIN' HEART:
SHOULD YOU BETRAY A BETRAYER?

You're at a restaurant having lunch with one of your sorority sisters from college, when you glance across the room and spot the husband of one of your best friends in an obviously romantic tête-à-tête with Another Woman. What do you do? Should you tell your friend—or keep your own counsel?

Experts are divided on this one, so don't be surprised to find yourself in a no-win situation. If you don't say anything, you may feel terribly burdened, a party to the betrayal. What's more, if your friend does find out that you know, she may well see your silence as a betrayal of her.

However, by telling her, you pit yourself against her spouse and run the risk of seriously compromising your friendship. What if she doesn't want to know? What if the evening you witnessed was merely a one-night fling, and your revelation destroys an otherwise solid marriage? She may mistrust your motives, she may no longer regard you as someone she can trust, and she may turn against you.

Remember, too, this type of situation holds the potential for becoming the basis of an unwitting betrayal, depending on how your friend perceives it. Unless she is already suspicious of her husband, and has asked you to let her know if you witness any infidelity on his part, before saying anything you should ask yourself why you feel compelled to tell in the first place. What are your true motives? Are you trying to alleviate your own guilt? Look carefully at the history of the marriage *and* the history of your friendship. Are you trying to save your friend pain? Are you taking any satisfaction from the situation—be careful of "I told you so." This way, whatever you decide to do, you will be in a position to make your friend understand that you care, and you then can discuss frankly what you expect from each other. If your friend's marriage is in trouble, she'll need your love and support.

SECTION II

The Many Faces of Betrayal

CHAPTER 4

Rivals: "I'm the Best"

Melissa and Carly had been best friends since their senior year in high school. "We were like sisters," said Melissa, twenty-five, a secretary in a travel agency. "If I needed to talk to anyone, I'd call Carly. If I needed a favor, she'd be there for me, and I'd be there for her." But their seven-year friendship came to an abrupt end when Melissa discovered that Carly had been having a two-month affair with Melissa's boyfriend, Gary, the man she'd expected to marry.

"I refused to believe it when another girlfriend told me," Melissa recalled. "I was in shock. Sure, Gary and I had been having problems, but I hoped we'd be able to work things out. In fact, I'd talked endlessly to Carly about Gary. She knew everything about us and I hate her for stealing him away . . ." she said, her voice trailing off. "But what hurts the most is that my best friend for seven years could do this to me. That betrayal is even more painful than losing Gary. It means our whole friendship was a lie."

But Carly didn't think she was doing anything wrong. "How could she say I betrayed her?" she said. "Didn't she tell me a thousand times she never wanted to see him again? For months, I listened to one gripe after another about Gary. She didn't want to be with him, anyway; why is she so surprised that we all got the message, too?"

Melissa and Carly's conflict represents a classic case of rivalry, perhaps the most common form of betrayal. Rivals are driven to compete and to challenge, to take away and take over what someone else has. Fueled by jealousy and propelled by deep insecurity and a lack of self-worth, rivals need to one-up or out-do anyone they view as a competitor or threat. This need to be the victor—at times they'll stop at nothing to achieve their goal—is the essence of rivalry.

Rivalries make headlines. We are appalled to read about the lengths to which people will go to hold on to a superior position. There's the beauty queen in West Virginia who tried to kill the woman who stole the man she loved . . . the Texas mother so consumed by the need to see her daughter make the high school cheerleading squad that she plotted to injure her chief competitor . . . the Olympic figure skater who allegedly connived to injure her rival so that she couldn't compete in the championships. In fact, one reason we are so attracted to such sordid stories is that there's a touch of rivalry in all of us. On some level, we can all identify with the desire to win at all costs. However, most of us are guided by a sense of fair play, which keeps our competitive, rivalrous feelings in check. It's hard to fathom how jealousy could drive a person to take such extreme measures.

GAMES PEOPLE PLAY

Rivalries spring up in any relationship—between best friends, business partners and colleagues, brothers and sisters, mothers and daughters—though we see them most often in the obviously competitive arenas of work and romance. Rivalries can even invade a marriage—celebrity marriages often fail for this very reason—when the spouses compare professional achievements to such a degree that they are no longer able to celebrate each other's triumphs. As compassion and empathy fall by the wayside, every encounter becomes a duel or contest. Who does more work around the house? Whose childrearing advice is best? Who gets to make the important decisions?

Rivalries begin in the family of origin, but they certainly don't remain there. Unresolved, they may be unconsciously carried over and repeated in every other relationship a person has. Then, too, with divorce, remarriage, and reconstructed families, many people are continuously subjected to feelings of displacement and replacement. In new family constellations, loyalties may be divided and rivalries can run rampant; a child may become intensely possessive of the remaining parent or bitterly jealous of a new step-parent or step-sibling.

That's what happened to Janet, a divorced mother of two, and her older daughter, Kristen, sixteen. When Janet and her husband divorced, both she and Kristen dealt with the loss of the man in their lives by competing with each other at every turn. Who was thinner? Who told the funniest jokes? Who attracted more male attention when they went shopping? Unconsciously, each was wrestling with a sense of abandonment that left her feeling worthless. By forever upping the ante, each was, in effect, saying, "See, since I'm the best, clearly he didn't leave because of me." The mother-daughter rivalry heated to the point that every issue became a confrontation; it even affected Janet's relationship with her new boyfriend, since Kristen flirted ceaselessly with him. By the time Janet sought counseling, she and her daughter were barely speaking.

Bitter rivalries crop up in the workplace when people, driven by the need to win, spread disparaging rumors about co-workers or sabotage their efforts. Jerry and Chris worked in the same radio station for several years, and Jerry considered his colleague a good friend. When Jerry applied for a job as executive producer at another station he confided in Chris and asked if it was okay to give him as a reference.

"I thought I had a really good chance of landing this new job," Jerry explained. "It was pretty much in the bag. All they wanted was a work reference, so naturally I gave them Chris's name." He was bitterly disappointed to learn the job had been offered to someone else—and stunned to discover, when he called to find out what had gone wrong, that Chris, instead of giving the favorable reference he had expected, had made several negative comments about him.

"Though he was outwardly supportive, I see now that Chris didn't want me to get the better job," said Jerry once the initial sting of betrayal wore off. "It's a small industry, and I'll bet he just couldn't handle the idea of me being a notch or two higher than him. I thought I knew the guy and could trust him, but clearly my judgment was way off."

Some interactions between friends become competitive and rivalrous in a more subtle way, especially when the critical trust factor discussed in Chapter 1—the expectation that someone will always be there for you—is challenged. Ronnie and Mara were best friends and apartment mates when they moved to Detroit after finishing graduate school. They both worked long hours in their respective jobs during the week—often on Saturdays, too—and looked forward to their regular Sunday routine: sleeping late, buying the newspaper, and having a leisurely brunch at a favorite café near a local park. That is, until Mara met Barry.

Mara didn't like her friend's new lover, and she didn't hesitate to say so. "I tried to like him, but I just didn't think he was right for her," Mara declared. "I thought she was making a big mistake, but when I tried to tell her—she'd always listened to my advice before—it created this incredible tension between us." Nevertheless, Mara insisted, she was happy for her friend, though, when pressed, she grudgingly acknowledged that she desperately missed the long chats and relaxed time they used to spend together. "I know she still cares about me, and we'll always be friends," Mara said, as if trying to convince herself. "But if I'm honest, I'd also say I felt ignored, left out, and, yes, betrayed."

A very close friend often has trouble accepting the other's lover or new spouse because it makes her feel insecure and replaced in her friend's life. Someone else has the unlimited access to a friend's time and attention she once had. Cynthia experienced such rivalrous feelings when Sybil, her girlhood friend, had her first child. "Even though we'd gone to different colleges, and now lived in different cities, I always knew I could pick up the phone and it would be as if we'd just spoken to each other yesterday," Cynthia remembered. "But now that Sybil's a mother, it's totally different. It's as if she's entered a different world, one I know nothing about. Every time we make plans, she changes them for one reason or another. She'll tell me to call her at a certain time, but then she can't talk because the baby's crying. We'll plan on seeing a show, and she'll cancel at the last minute because she can't get a sitter. I know she expects me to understand, and I try to, but I keep feeling that I can't depend on her anymore. Okay, I know she's tired, but can't she at least finish a phone conversation? How about asking me something about my life?" Cynthia wants to know. "It sounds ridiculous," she added, "but I suppose I'm actually jealous of a six-month-old."

Mara's and Cynthia's reactions do seem embarrassingly trivial and selfish at first, but they are not uncommon. Many people feel abandoned whenever a close friend or loved one appears to place her interest and allegiance in someone else. Situations and roles may change—through marriage, divorce, the birth of a baby, or a promotion at work—but the expectation of availability that others often have remains constant. This can trigger miscommunication, smoldering resentment, and even raw feelings of anger and jealousy. The result: all-out battles and the unsettling feeling that a once-trusted friend is no longer there for you. Indeed, though Ronnie and Sybil have legitimate reasons for their actions, Mara and Cynthia experience their behavior as betrayal. Swamped by rivalrous competition they scarcely recognize and barely understand, they express their feelings in terms of disapproval and outrage. Few relationships, let alone a close friendship, can withstand such competition.

Ian is another example of someone who felt displaced, although he didn't realize it. Six months ago, Ian introduced Kenny, his best friend, to his younger sister, Barbara, a divorced mother of two. Since Barbara's marriage had fallen apart, Ian had grown so close to his sister and her children, often joining them for dinner during the week and spending weekend afternoons, that he felt more like a surrogate father than a beloved uncle.

But as Kenny and Barbara grew closer, Ian became anxious and angry. When they announced their engagement, he blew up. "I'm furious at Ken, furious at Barbara. I feel betrayed," he announced, the anger rising in his voice. Ian's was a compounded loss: his role as number one across the board had vanished. No longer did he feel like the main man in his sister's eyes, the substitute dad for his nieces, or the best friend in Kenny's life. He knew Kenny was good for Barbara and her kids; but, deep down, he believed he was better.

WHAT'S IT ALL ABOUT?

The roots of rivalry—as well as how we react to it—run deep. As I discussed in Chapter 1, our childhood experiences influence our adult perceptions and behaviors, often propelling us into relationships—with lovers, husbands, friends, or colleagues—in which we continue to play out those early dynamics. For many people, unresolved Oedipal issues, as well as lingering sibling rivalries, have a decided impact on their view of themselves as well as on any relationships they may enter into in the future.

Simply put, a child around three to five years of age, once

he has separated emotionally from his parents or primary caregiver and formed a sense of his own identity, begins to view the world from a three-person rather than a two-person perspective. This emotional triangle of mother, father, and child—what Freud first termed the Oedipus complex—can trigger intense feelings of love, hatred, and jealousy. According to Freud, a child develops a strong erotic drive for the parent of the opposite sex, and unconsciously competes as a rival with the same-sex parent for the other parent's love. In fact, Freud suggested, a child is so consumed with rivalrous feelings that he, again unconsciously, wants to eliminate the same-sex parent, much like Oedipus, the character in Aeschylus' Greek tragedy, who kills his father and falls in love with his mother.

Developmentally, Oedipal issues first occur when a child is between three and five. They are revived at puberty, and ordinarily surmounted with varying degrees of success, when an individual learns to identify in a positive way with the same-sex parent. In adulthood, then, a person often seeks a partner who possesses the attributes of the opposite-sex parent. The lyrics to the old song, "I want a girl, just like the girl, who married dear old Dad," perfectly sum up the successful resolution of childhood Oedipal issues. However, for many people, early Oedipal relationships are revisited with a vengeance, and triangulated relationships begin to take precedence.

Valerie is a good example of someone who is still struggling with unresolved Oedipal issues. The vice president of a major national bank, Valerie had risen swiftly through the ranks. However, though meticulous and successful at work, she was unable to judge the trustworthiness of friends. A look back at her life illustrates a series of emotional losses that compromised her ability to feel secure in her judgment and left her vulnerable to repeated abandonments.

Valerie experienced her first loss with the sudden death of her father, when she was nine. Over the next few years, she developed an extremely close relationship with her mother, one that was more friend than mother-daughter; she even shared a bedroom with her mother after graduating from college and moving back home. But when Valerie's mother remarried, Valeric, at twenty-one, felt—indeed, was—pushed aside. Though she never acknowledged her sad or jealous feelings, they influenced her actions at every turn.

As we talked, I reflected that Valerie didn't realize how clear the picture of repeated betrayal in her life really was. In high school, she told me, her best friend had flirted, and finally wooed away, her boyfriend. At her first job, she had assumed the young woman she shared many lunches with was a confidante, only to discover that she had been gossiping behind her back to others in the office. And just recently, Valerie was betrayed by Margot, a woman she had met at the gym and whom she considered a close friend.

"I can't believe this really happened," she began as she walked into my office. "I trusted Margot with all my heart. She's not very attractive, so I really didn't see her as a threat. I assumed she cared as much for me as I did for her, that she took my interests to heart as much as I did hers."

That's why Valerie asked Margot to meet Craig, the new man in her life. "I really liked Craig, a lot," Valerie explained, "but things were happening too fast for me. I'd just ended a bad relationship, and I didn't trust my own intuition or judgment of men. I felt I needed Margot to give me a second opinion, so to speak, to tell me if she thought Craig was as special as I did."

Margot did think Craig was special. So special, in fact, that several weeks later when Valerie was out of town on a business trip, and Craig called to ask Margot to have a drink with him after work, she ended up sleeping with him.

Clearly, Valerie had woefully underestimated the competition Margot represented. Once again, she found herself the odd man out in an emotional triangle, with both a betraying girlfriend and a two-timing boyfriend.

We can see the outlines of another triangulated relationship in the story of Jenny, Ellen, and Ethan. Jenny and Ellen were roommates and best friends at college. You couldn't have found two people who were more different: blond, soft-spoken Jenny, who had grown up in a religious home in the Midwest, and smart-alecky Ellen, a tough-talking girl from Staten Island, New York. Still, they bonded instantly during freshmen orientation week. In fact, the two women, and Jenny's boyfriend, Ethan, became a threesome that year, spending nearly all their free time together.

"We all love each other so much," Ellen said. So why, then, did she sleep with Ethan? Ellen stammered out her explanation: "Well, we got drunk, and were just fooling around. One thing led to another. Jenny's a virgin, and I'm not. Well, it just happened, and I feel so guilty, but it really didn't mean anything."

Perhaps it didn't to Ellen. But Jenny was devastated. She didn't know how to respond to a betrayal by the two people she loved most in the world. "They're like my family," she said softly. "I don't know what to do. I can't imagine not having them in my life."

Melissa, Jerry, Valerie, and Jenny were all betrayed by rivals they believed they could trust. As you will see in subsequent chapters, each ultimately chose a different course of action to right a perceived wrong: Melissa opted for revenge; Jerry chose not to confront Chris; Valerie chose never to speak to Margot again; and Jenny decided to forgive her betrayers. In Section III, I'll discuss the reasons for, as well as the repercussions of, these actions. Meanwhile, let's take a look at another trigger for rivalrous relationships.

THE SIBLING WARS

The intense feelings generated by sibling conflicts are as significant as Oedipal issues in determining how we respond to rivals in our later relationships. The quick-as-lightning childhood squabbles over who goes first or who pushed whom—accompanied by shouts and whines—are a vital part of a child's emotional and social development. Staged to attract parents' attention and aimed at prompting their action, sibling warfare is really about getting your fair share—of love, attention, and security. Even an only child is affected to some degree by the competition for his parents' attention from aunts, uncles, or other family members.

As I noted in my first book, *Adult Sibling Rivalry*, a child who sees a sibling get more attention from Mom and Dad may think, "She's worth more than I am." In a child's mind, if a sibling has something the other doesn't, that must mean she's more loved and more valued. Children often confuse feeling "worth less" to their parents with feeling inherently worthless, creating within them a hollow place that needs to be filled. Self-esteem becomes based not on what a child has and can accomplish, but on what she doesn't have and wishes she did. In the future, she may find that she is constantly measuring herself against others—and coming up short.

What's more, the way parents respond to sibling battles, and the way they teach children to handle them, cast a long shadow over the ways people respond to conflict and rivalry later on. Did Mom and Dad favor one child over another? Did they make comparisons between them? Did they admonish siblings with the reprimand *Brothers (or sisters) shouldn't fight!*— when, in fact, sibling friction is normal, indeed, healthy?

Coming to terms with the powerful feelings triggered by unresolved Oedipal and sibling issues marks a critical passage in a child's psychological development. When early rivalry issues are resolved in a healthy way, people learn a great deal about themselves as well as how to channel aggressive competitive feelings in appropriate ways. Most important, they learn to handle the disappointment of losing or the pain of rejection without having their self-esteem and self-worth demolished. They can bounce back from failure and learn from their mistakes, whether in school, at work, or in their relationships.

However, when sibling rivalry is unchecked, it's almost impossible for children to gain a sense of fair play. Disappointment breeds anger, contempt, jealousy, and the desire to take away what a rival has. What's more, in the absence of parental limit-setting, children cannot develop a respect for the rights or possessions of others. In fact, they may never learn to discriminate between helping themselves to a brother's model airplane—or, later, luring away another's lover or spouse.

Indeed, long-ago experiences of sibling rivalry affect people in different ways as they attempt, usually unconsciously, to address old grievances and heal old hurts. If a person felt one-down as a child, she may need to feel one-up as an adult. To settle the score, she may continue to compete with a sibling, even as an adult, for who has the better job, the bigger house, the smarter kids.

The events that tore apart the Brant family illustrate the ramifications of rivalrous betrayal between siblings. Doreen and Jeff Brant had been married for five unhappy years, and their inability to talk openly and honestly with each other was exacerbated by constant financial strain. When Jeff was laid off from his midlevel managerial job in Denver, they decided to move back home to Wyoming to be nearer to his family. Jeff's older brother, Howard, had offered him a job in his small insurance company, Jeff explained, "and we hoped that being back home, near the family, would give us the fresh start we badly needed."

But the move proved disastrous for the marriage. The recently divorced Howard had an affair with Doreen, and, after a bitter break with the family, the two were married and now have a child of their own.

"How the hell could he do this?" Jeff said, describing the deception. "Howard knew my wife and I were having problems, and he took advantage. He moved right in."

The fallout of Howard's betrayal had a particularly harsh effect on Meg, now thirty-five, Jeff and Howard's youngest sister, who had always worshiped her oldest brother. "Howie was my hero," Meg recalled. "Ever since I was little, I was the apple of his eye, his favorite. He always paid much more attention to me than he ever did to my other two sisters. But as soon as Doreen came along, he forgot about me." Even though

Meg was also married, with two small children of her own, she still felt jealous, hurt, and betrayed. She hasn't spoken to Howard or Doreen in nine years.

"I want the family to be whole again," Meg said wistfully. "Maybe someday it'll be possible, but right now, there's too much pain and too much hurt." Howard, for his part, vacillates between feeling guilty about "stealing" his brother's wife and feeling the need to justify his actions. "I know that good Christians aren't adulterers," he said with a shrug. "But Doreen and Jeff's marriage wasn't right from the start. You can't steal someone who doesn't want to be stolen. I know people were hurt, but it couldn't be helped."

THE INVISIBLE SIBLING

Rivalrous feelings may also be triggered by what I identified in *Adult Sibling Rivalry* as the Invisible Sibling—that is, someone other than a brother or sister whose presence in your life evokes the old feelings, positive as well as negative, of childhood sibling issues. For Meg Brant, her sister-in-law Doreen was the invisible sibling. Even as a grown woman, Meg was, in effect, still competing for the love and affection of her older brother. When Doreen and Howard married, and dropped virtually all contact with the rest of the family, Meg felt displaced; all the rivalrous feelings she had experienced as a child with her own sisters resurfaced.

Sometimes, competition and rivalry are even passed from one generation to another. Take the case of Abby, whose relationship with her first cousin Robin, the daughter of her mother's sister, was punctuated by rivalry. The two families lived in the same town, and the girls' mothers had long been locked in a bitter sibling rivalry of their own. Trying to one-up each other at every opportunity, they continued the battle through and with their daughters. Which girl was smarter? Prettier? Who dated first? Who was accepted into the better college?

"My mother was mean and controlling with me, but she lived in fear of her older sister," Abby recalled. "She made me just as afraid of doing anything to upset my cousin Robin. I was always told to let things roll off my back, never to speak up and say my piece, because if I did, they'd be mad at me and wouldn't like me anymore."

Though the mothers' rivalry was obvious to all, Robin and Abby tried to bury their feelings and to maintain, at least on the surface, a semblance of friendship. But time and again their relationship was put to severe tests. Abby recalls a particularly difficult time when she was pregnant with her first child. "I had gained sixty-five pounds, and I knew that was way too much. Robin, an obstetrical nurse who was not married and had no children of her own, never missed an opportunity to criticize me for it. She even tried to seduce my husband. Then, after I had the baby, and was a very nervous new mom, she needled me constantly about the difficulty I was having trying to breastfeed my son." But even after Abby regained her emotional footing, she never said anything to her cousin about her hurtful and undermining behavior. The two are on apparently cordial but really cold terms.

It's important to note that the mixture of negative feelings stemming from both Oedipal and sibling rivalry may be frightening to a child, but they aren't all bad. In fact, competition spurs ambition, and energizes a person to set goals and strive to reach them. The question is: Where does the line between normal, healthy competitive rivalry end, and destructive, self-consuming rivalry begin?

THE CORROSIVE POWER
OF JEALOUSY

Too often, one of the byproducts of the inability to work through Oedipal and siblings issues is a fundamental lack of self-confidence that makes a person quick to experience jealous feelings in many areas. In fact, jealousy is one kind of armor people use to protect themselves from the loss of someone or something they love. Whenever we feel our essential being is threatened—whether someone is flirting with our spouse or pitching for the job we believe we deserve—we feel jealous.

People who lack self-confidence believe that they don't have what it takes to hold their own in the face of a rival. What's more, they feel vulnerable to, or fearful of, someone better coming along and snatching what they do have. For this reason, when they lose a beauty pageant, a position, or a lover to a rival, the loss is staggering—far greater than the loss of the actual person or job. Rather, it is what that person or job represents. The loss becomes a confirmation of personal failure, as if they've been exposed as a fraud. If they are prone to angry outbursts, the loss may be equivalent to a lit match on a stick of dynamite; they explode with acts of retaliation and revenge.

While everyone feels jealousy from time to time, they usually learn to bridle or channel it. The experience may even spur them on to do better and achieve more. And when they accomplish something in their own right, they develop self-confidence and a tougher skin, which can help them withstand future threats.

When people feel insecure and inadequate, however, the threat that something valuable will be taken away may drive them to irrational behavior. Fueled by rivalrous jealousy, they may connive, gossip, manipulate, deceive, cheat, and ultimately betray whoever is in the way of their gaining and/or retaining the number one spot. Instead of telling you directly how they feel, they indulge in backstabbing behavior, motivated by the need to make you lose face. Their aim is not to give you constructive advice but to tear you down. Rivals may feel so self-righteous that their anger, their need for revenge, takes on a life of its own—a phenomenon I'll discuss in Chapter 7.

WILLING VICTIMS?
YOUR RISK FACTORS

Over and over again, in love and in work, you meet the rival who pushes you out of the way or steps on you in his quest to get ahead. Yet in my practice I encounter many people who simply don't realize how they repeatedly set themselves up for such betrayals. Like Valerie, you may find yourself blindsided by those you counted as friends, supporters, or confidantes. Can you learn to protect yourself?

The answer is yes—but first you must understand the risk factors that make you emotionally vulnerable to breaches of trust by all potential betrayers, be they Rivals, Admirers, or Users, whom we will meet in later chapters. While the first two risk factors discussed below are applicable to all types of betrayers, numbers three and four are specific to Rivals. Let them serve as a warning signal.

Risk Factor #1: You Have a History of Betrayals in Your Life

For Valerie, one betrayal followed another, though she never realized it, and when I pointed out the pattern, she was genuinely taken aback. She kept giving people the benefit of the doubt. By doing so, she never had to confront them with her anger; instead, she let her betrayers off the hook. Although each betrayal wounded her deeply, it was of the moment. At the time, it seemed she would never live through it, but she did—and, rather quickly, put the event behind her. What's more, she never looked back. As a result, every betrayal was a new one, and it hit hard. Each time, she repeated the cycle of shock and pain. Each time, she vowed never to see or speak to her rival again. Yet as soon as her anger dissipated, she would resume the relationship and naïvely assume that the person would never betray her again. Or she would enter a new relationship without giving herself sufficient time to process the emotional damage she had sustained.

Do you find yourself falling into similar situations? Take stock. Ask yourself: Has this happened before? Something about your current problem may indeed be similar to a past event, situation, or relationship. Look again at the sandtraps described in Chapter Two. Distinguish which ones may be guiding your assumptions about yourself and others, leaving you wide open to betrayal.

Risk Factor #2:
You've Been Abandoned by
Significant People in Your Life

We all experience the feeling of being abandoned, in varying degrees, as we grow up. But for some people, the losses of childhood are profound and constant. Valerie, for example, first felt abandoned when her father died. When her mother remarried, those painful feelings were rekindled. From that day on, she fought to be number one in every relationship, with a friend or a lover.

Could this be happening in your life? Take an inventory of your childhood. Did any close family members die or move away? Was the family torn apart by a bitter divorce? Were any close family members victims of drug or alcohol abuse? Such experiences may have left you acutely sensitive to loss and wary of anyone—the friend of a friend, the newcomer at work— who threatens what you have. If you've sustained any of these losses, you may have the need to prove your worth, to compete in order to feel victorious and undo the previous loss. It may leave you open to betrayal as you seek to heal old wounds through new relationships. Or it may cause you to betray someone else. After all, if you're the best, you'll never be left again.

Risk Factor #3:
Three's Company Is a Way of Life

People who often find themselves in three-way relationships—emotional triangles, like Melissa and Carly or like Jenny, Ellen, and Ethan—are particularly vulnerable to betrayals. As long as emotional boundaries are respected, a three-way relationship, though it can be a problem, may still work. However, if you feel twinges of jealousy, don't be naïve: a three-way relationship has the potential to self-destruct at any time. It can readily fall prey to two-timing, two-faced behavior, which divides a threesome into fragments.

Look closely at the patterns of your encounters and conflicts with others. Pay attention to any uneasiness you may be experiencing; you may need to set limits to protect yourself, which you'll learn how to do in Chapter 10. Ask yourself honestly whether you are often moved to share your time, your possessions, your creative ideas. Do you ever wonder whether you are giving too much and getting too little in return?

Consider, too, the possibility that unresolved Oedipal issues from childhood may emerge not only for you but also for other members of the triangle, at any point in your three-way relationship. If this happens, you must learn to confront and resolve them in a healthy way, which I discuss in Chapter 8.

Risk Factor #4:
You Must Be Number One

Bluntly assess your personal style. Are you fiercely competitive? Consider how others seem to perceive you. Are your friendships fleeting? Are colleagues resentful? You may feel that someone is getting more than you at work or in love; more money, more attention; that he is the "favorite child." You may often fear that your position is threatened. Recognizing that you have an Achilles' heel will alert you to someone who may be out to do you in.

Whether you are currently getting along well, fighting with, or even if you haven't seen or spoken to a sibling in years, that old rivalry may still be affecting you. In fact, surprising numbers of people are oblivious of obvious similarities until they are pointed out to them. Like Abby, as well as members of the Brant family, you may find yourself struggling with someone who reminds you, emotionally or physically, of a brother or sister. Perhaps he or she is similar in age, appearance and name, or holds a similar job. The familiarity can drive you to act, in ways that puzzle you, so that you come out on top. Perhaps you may even behave in betraying ways. What you don't realize is that you are feeling competition with an invisible sibling.

Think about the way you react to people in your life now. Are you responding with sadness, anger, rage, or feelings of unworthiness, much as you did when you were younger? It's not uncommon for friends, colleagues, or spouses to evoke earlier feelings of jealousy and resentment that propel you to prove you really are the best. By positioning yourself in such a rivalrous relationship, you are attempting to rewrite the script so that this time you're the winner.

SURE WAYS TO SPOT A RIVAL

- They always one-up you. You tell them your son made honor roll; they tell you theirs is valedictorian. Be alert: one-upmanship may occur even in seemingly negative situations. You tell your friend that your child was up all night with an earache; she'll report that hers had strep throat and a temperature of 103°.
- They make themselves look good by putting you down. Your kids, your spouse, are all grist for their put-down mill.
- They constantly compare themselves with you. Their conversations are peppered with personal questions that make you feel not flattered but uneasy: What did you buy at the department store sale? Where did you eat last weekend in the city? How much do people at your level get paid?
- They fail to back you up at work, with friends, or with family members. When someone criticizes you, instead of offering support or countering the comments, they remain silent.
- They punch holes in your balloon and rain on your parade. "Why did you cut your hair?" they'll ask. "It looked so good long." "You're going to that restaurant? The last time I was there, it really wasn't very good."

QUICK TIP: WHAT YOU CAN DO
TO REBUFF A RIVAL

If you can confront a rival early on and set limits, you may be able to avert a betrayal and get the relationship back on an even keel. For more information, consult the confrontation strategies in Chapter 8 as well as the guidelines for setting limits in Chapter 10.

Instead of challenging your rival, pose a question to let her know that you know what she's doing. You might say, "Why do you always have to compare yourself to me? Do you realize that every comment you make to me is a negative one?"

CHAPTER 5

Admirers: "You're the Best"

We all have people in our lives whom we look up to—parents, older siblings, teachers, friends, mentors, celebrities, or heroes. These people inspire, motivate, and encourage us. We identify with them, respect them, internalize their qualities, and, to some degree, forge our own identity in their image. We turn to them for their wisdom, and model our behavior, attitudes, and values after theirs. They represent everything good and powerful to us, and we aspire to the traits they possess: their intelligence and accomplishments, their attractiveness, their strength, their sense of humor.

In a healthy adult relationship, admiration is reciprocal. You mirror the best in each other, bring out the best in each other, and the relationship is based on mutual appreciation and respect; in other words, there's something in it for both of you. You feel proud of the other person, and appreciate that he is equally proud of you. However, an admiring relationship can be a double-edged sword. The mutuality that sustains it may also make it tricky.

Just as there is a line between healthy rivalry and destructive jealousy, there is a line between healthy admiration and envy—between someone wanting to be like you and wanting to be you—between longing for what you have and claiming what you have. As long as both people admire, and are admired, equally, all is well. But when one person's admiration turns to envy, it may be only a matter of time before the relationship deteriorates, and the person you admire, respect, and think you can trust disappoints or deceives you. When you are dealing with an Admirer, you must be on guard for the subtle shift; it's the point at which you are most vulnerable to betrayal.

Unlike jealousy, which springs from the fear that someone else will take away a person or a thing that is a source of love and nurturance, envy is based on a deep sense of deprivation, the desperate yearning for something someone has. Inherent in that definition is the belief that if she has something you do not, then you must be inadequate or lacking in a fundamental way. Many experts believe that envy is on the rise: while other generations had a sense that life posed limitations, most baby boomers were weaned on the belief that they could have it all if they only went after it. The hard lesson of the nineties is, quite simply, that there isn't enough of anything—good jobs, high salaries, creative talent—to go around. Thwarted in their expectations, many people nurse their sense of life's unfairness, and unless that feeling is bridled, they may stop at nothing to get what they believe they are entitled to.

WITH MALICE TOWARD ALL

The blind spot for many is that they continue to trust an Admirer, not recognizing that his or her feelings may have changed to those of intense envy. Consequently, a healthy relationship subtly shifts from being one of mutual admiration to one tinged or propelled by envy. Even the most discerning people find it difficult to detect the change in time to protect themselves. Whereas Rivals want to take away what you have and leave you empty-handed, Admirers want to acquire what you have. Their motto: "What's yours should also be mine."

An admirer doesn't necessarily wish you harm. She simply wants to be you, and to inherit all that you possess. You welcome an Admirer into your life because, as your biggest fan, she makes you feel good, enhancing your self-esteem tenfold. Basking in her adulation, you're willing to do all that you can to help her and merit their praise. And remember: you also admire her for her accomplishments and feel that she enhances your life as well. By pooling your resources, you form a power pact; you both feel strong.

However, if the scale tips too much, you are likely to feel betrayed. This is what happened to Helen, an account executive in an advertising agency. When Helen hired Kimberly as an associate in her department, she was impressed by the younger woman's intelligence and enthusiasm. Helen invested a tremendous amount of time and energy helping Kimberly learn the field—she introduced her to key people in the company, included her in meetings, and even gave her access to her Rolodex.

Clearly, she was grooming her to manage the department when she traveled on business. Kimberly seemed more than grateful: she admired Helen and often marveled at her ability to do so much and still be so kind and helpful to others. Helen was flattered when she noticed the way Kimberly emulated her clothes and hairstyle—and chuckled when colleagues told her that her new assistant was even beginning to sound like her when she answered the phone. She reminded Helen of her younger sister, Gillian, with whom she had always yearned to be close but who had rejected her help and encouragement.

Over the next few months, Helen took pride in her talented young discovery and often steered plum assignments Kimberly's way. She paid little attention to the small things that, in hindsight, ought to have given her a clearer picture of the young woman's intentions. At one department meeting, for instance, Helen left the room to answer a phone call. Kimberly literally took her seat, right next to the creative director. "I dismissed that," Helen says, thinking back. "I just figured she wanted a closer look at the story boards he was showing us."

Needless to say, Helen was horrified to learn that Kimberly had secretly gone to Helen's boss and pitched herself as more suited than Helen to handle a certain account. Ultimately, Kimberly won the coveted account, was promoted to be on a par with Helen, and moved into the office across the hall.

"To tell you the truth, my head is still spinning," Helen admitted. "I feel so duped. I never for a minute believed that Kimberly would do such a thing. She always seemed to have my best interests at heart. Besides, she had so much to lose by alienating me."

FASTEN YOUR SEATBELTS;
IT'S GOING TO BE A BUMPY RIDE

As Helen discovered, an Admirer may be the person you mentor at work, who behind your back wrangles for a promotion that should rightly be yours. She may be the shy new neighbor you brought into your social circle, only to learn that she has begun an affair with your husband. Or he may be the fraternity brother from college who innocently flirts with the woman you're dating and eventually steals her away.

Unlike Rivals, whose motto is "May the best man win," Admirers are the people who look up to you, insist you're the best—and then step on you in their quest to be as good if not better. This dynamic was made exquisitely clear in the classic Bette Davis film *All About Eve.* When Davis's character, Margo Channing, a Broadway star at the apex of her career, describes her new adoring assistant, the conniving Eve Harrington, to her fiancé, she says, "She thinks of me all the time; it's flattering." Whereupon her fiancé replies, "She thinks about you . . . she's studying you."

Indeed, flattery is the Admirers' bait; with it, they hook you into doing things for them while they gobble up your energy and your possessions, and step into your world.

Why do some people yearn so deeply for admiration that they will do anything to get it? Why are others so gullible that they consistently fail to discriminate between people whose praise and admiration are genuine, and those whose ulterior motives lead them to betray a trust? The roots of both these needs lie in a person's childhood and the development of what experts call the narcissistic personality. A narcissist may easily betray a trust because, first, he feels he has a right to. Indeed, for the narcissist, it is necessary for him to do whatever it is he is doing, regardless of the impact of his actions, because his needs are all that count. Second, he may genuinely have no idea that he is violating a boundary, since he experiences whatever belongs to you as his, too.

Narcissism is defined as self-love, or any intense, excessive interest in one's own appearance, comfort, importance, or needs. The name derives from Narcissus, the young god in Greek mythology who haughtily rejected legions of admirers and, as punishment, was destined to gaze lovingly at his reflection in the still waters of a pond until he wasted away and died. According to the theorist Heinz Kohut, whose work in the 1960s focused on these issues, narcissists often overestimate their abilities and inflate their accomplishments. Boastful and pretentious, they believe their needs are more urgent than everyone else's and their achievements greater; they have little patience for the feelings, needs, or concerns of others. Narcissists are the people who must have the "best" doctor in the city, whose child goes to the "best" school, whose choice of vacation spot is always tops, bar none.

Yet despite the narcissists' outward show, their self-esteem is quite fragile. As Kohut noted, they are frequently preoccupied with how well they are doing and what others think of them. They crave attention and register shock and surprise when the praise they believe they deserve is not forthcoming. Overly sensitive to failures, disappointments, and slights, they seek the approval of others in order to maintain their self-esteem.

It's important to note that a certain degree of narcissism is normal and healthy: it's important to be pleased with yourself and proud of your accomplishments. When you are, you're also able to enjoy sincerely the achievements of others. However, when the emotional needs of childhood have not been met, there remains the potential for unbalanced relationships, and the stage is set for betrayal.

As I discussed in Chapter 1, parents play a major role in helping a child develop a strong sense of self-worth and the belief that others will be there for him. They are also instrumental in two ways in the formation of healthy narcissism. Parents are a child's first heroes. He idealizes them and tries to emulate their strengths, wisdom, and power. In the early years, a child does not have a sense of boundary and separateness between himself and the powerful other (usually the mother) who supplies him with love and affection. As a result, he is "one" with her and shares a sense of omnipotence with her.

Over time, this grandiosity is tamed both by social constraints and a child's mastery of his own world. However, if it is not tempered, unconsciously a child is unable to separate himself and his achievements from those of others. For a narcissist, this sense of oneness remains all-consuming; it's a small step from seeing what another has and owns to what he then matter-of-factly claims as his.

For this reason, narcissists exude a sense of entitlement. They believe they should have exactly what you have. From this feeling of righteousness springs the contempt that propels Admirers toward self-serving and exploitive behavior. They may idealize you and, at the same time, devalue you if you fail to support them in the way they expect. Not only do narcissists think that what you do is easy; they're convinced they can do it just as well.

Parents may also unwittingly foster narcissism when they fail to act as a mirror that reflects a child's unique talents, traits, and abilities. In the best of all possible worlds, parents acknowledge how proud they are of a child's achievements. "Mommy, watch me, watch me," a child shouts as he rides his two-wheeler for the first time or attempts a dive off the high board. When Mommy exclaims in joy, "Good for you! That was great!" a child develops a sense of pride, self-confidence, and self-reliance. But if a parent is not attentive to a child's accomplishments, he begins to feel insecure and unsure of his abilities. If this much-needed early reinforcement is missing, a child will search for it elsewhere—often embarking on a life-long quest for attention and approval.

Indeed, a child's need for parental attention is critical not only in triumphant moments but also during times of disappointment. If the child falls off his bike, and Mommy is there to empathize with and soothe his pain, he soon learns to calm and soothe himself. If Mom is not around or fails to offer comfort, a child may be overwhelmed by anger and feelings of helplessness. He has no actual experience of relief or reassurance, and hence no model by which he can learn to feel better about his failures. He remains focused on how to alleviate his own distress and increase his own comfort. As an adult, he may be insensitive and oblivious of the pain and discomfort of others. Unable to empathize, he cannot fathom the ultimate impact of his actions. Just like the absent parent, he's unaware and doesn't care—yet another classic characteristic of the narcissist.

What Have You Done for Me Lately?

To get a better sense of how narcissism affects a relationship, let's take a close look at the six-year friendship of Myra and Sophia. Their relationship began with mutual admiration. However, in time, it deteriorated into a lopsided one, with Myra giving and admiring far more than she was getting. In fact, their seemingly loving relationship, which started when their sons were in pre-school, had been punctuated by betrayals for years, though Myra was oblivious of Sophia's callous disregard for her well-being, and held on to the expectation that friends reciprocate favors.

"We were like sisters," recalled Myra, an editor and writer who lives in a suburb of San Diego. "I loved her, loved her kids. I felt as if they were mine. We shared birthdays and holidays together. There wasn't a thing I wouldn't do for her. She made me feel like a million bucks, always telling me how smart I was, how helpful and how she could never manage her life without my support. Her praise meant the world to me."

Knowing that Sophia and her husband had financial problems, Myra lent her money, though things were certainly tight in her own home. She extended an open invitation to Sophia to come to dinner whenever she wanted. She campaigned for Sophia's son to get into a highly competitive academic program, and even recommended Sophia for a job when she heard of an opening at a local public relations firm. When Sophia's car was in the repair shop, Myra literally chauffered her around the city. She was always the one to pick up the phone and initiate plans. "Sophia never called to acknowledge what I had done or to thank me," Myra said. "So why did I keep doing it? Because it was the most natural thing in the world for me. Doing things for Sophia was never a burden; it was a joy. Her family was as dear to me as if it were my own. I mistakenly believed that she'd do the same for me."

And at times, it seems, she did. "I treasured our friendship. We shared everything—intimate details about our families, our marriages, our children. She always looked to me for the answers to show her the way. I felt so important. Sophia was the close family I had never had growing up. There have been a few friends in my life who have been like family to me, and Sophia was one of them." Often, this very real sense of belonging—akin to what you feel to your true family—fosters a feeling of responsibility that compounds your desire to do and give to an Admirer. Because you share such a history, an Admirer's failure to reciprocate is a painful betrayal. In fact, the lack of reciprocity is often the key point of contention in dealing with an Admirer.

Still, Myra admitted, she would periodically have fleeting thoughts that the friendship did not mean as much to Sophia as it did to her. Like the time Sophia refused to baby-sit for her son so that she could go on a job interview. Or the time she seemed less than overjoyed to hear about an important award Myra had won.

"I think I sensed on some level that the relationship wasn't mutual, but I dismissed all the obvious signs, and ignored her occasional coldness. I wouldn't let myself believe what was happening right in front of my nose," Myra said. Other friends would say, "Look how she's taking advantage of you! How can you make excuses for her?" But, explained Myra, "I gave her the benefit of the doubt. I never came out and said, 'How

could you do such a thing?' because I didn't want our relationship to end. She was that important to me."

Another feature of the Admirer is that she uses your power
to empower herself; when she no longer needs you, you become dispensable. Indeed, when Sophia applied for a part-
time job at the local newspaper, one that she knew Myra
wanted desperately and was clearly in line for, Myra could no
longer rationalize away the betrayal of trust.

Like others caught in a web of seemingly small betrayals,
Myra soon began to doubt her intuition and to question every
other relationship in her life. "I've always prided myself on my
good instincts," Myra said, "but this time, I felt I was sitting in
front of an oncoming train. I knew what I had to do—get out
of the way—but I couldn't bring myself to do it." Myra could
no longer trust her best friend. And she could no longer trust
herself.

When admiration turns lopsided, victims often feel as if the
wind has been knocked out of them. "It's been very painful;
I'm shattered," Myra admitted. "And I feel like an idiot, but I
can't get a handle on what to do. How could I have misjudged
her? And to make it worse, I still want desperately to be her
friend."

In time, Myra forced Sophia to discuss the deterioration of
their friendship. But when the conversation had ended, Myra,
not Sophia, was the one in tears. "When I finally asked her
why she always allowed me to do things for her but rarely vol-
unteered any help in return, she turned to me and said in
a perfectly even tone, 'Well, you offered.' It hit like a ton of
bricks," Myra said. "She felt entitled; she simply didn't care
about me at all and was, in fact, rewriting history and telling
me now that our whole friendship was a sham. That's what

hurts the most. She cut me off just like that. It was as if she'd decapitated me." Indeed, with the loss of such a friendship, you do feel you're losing part of yourself, since the essence of the admiring relationship is the oneness you feel with another.

Myra was an easy target for the narcissistic Sophia. Had she not been so desperate for the friendship and the sense of family it provided, she would have noticed that Sophia never gave of herself in any substantial way. Myra expected Sophia to reciprocate; however, a classic trait of the narcissist is that she never truly extends herself unless it's convenient for her. Sophia would offer to drop Myra's clothes at the dry cleaners *if* she was already making the trip. But if Myra asked her to go out of her way for her—for instance, when she asked her to watch her children so that she could go on a job interview— Sophia declined. She was "just so busy"; "It would be such an imposition." And Myra wound up feeling guilty that she had asked in the first place.

Narcissists like Sophia often appear to turn on a dime. Their needs are of the moment. Say no to them once, and everything you've ever done for them is instantly forgotten. All they know and feel is their current disappointment and anger. Consequently, they seem open, friendly, and loving one day, sulky and withdrawn the next if you fail to meet their requests, no matter how unreasonable they may be. Over time, they seem to be casting aside a relationship of long standing with nary an explanation. But, as far as they're concerned, their often unspoken resentment and grievances against you are perfectly legitimate. You're bewildered; you've done so much, but in their eyes, because they expected you to give unconditionally, you weren't there for them.

Admirers also wind up issuing promises they may plan to keep but never do. That's what happened to Eliot, a business-man, who counted on Barry, his childhood friend and an associate professor at a prestigious liberal arts college in the South, to write a letter of recommendation to the school for his son.

"I'd done a lot of favors for Barry over the years," Eliot recalled, "and when I called to ask him to help us, he told me not to give it a second thought. He assured me that he was good friends with the dean of admissions and that the letter was as good as written. When my son didn't get accepted, and we checked to find out what had gone wrong, we were shocked to learn that Barry had never even written," he said, his voice trailing off. "I still can't believe he deceived me that way."

Like Eliot, many people assume that a trusted friend will be there—perhaps to recommend them for a higher position or to make a phone call on their behalf. After all, they reason, I'd do the same for him. When the job offer never comes through, when the recommendation never gets written, or the phone call never gets made—they are astounded to dis-cover that someone they counted on overestimated their im-portance, abilities, or connections. Even worse, they may find out that their "friend" simply didn't want to waste a favor on them. "It wasn't my fault," an Admirer will say, as he tries to explain why he failed to honor a promise. "There was nothing I could do."

And so, what begins as mutual admiration disintegrates into self-serving admiration. The person with the most to start with—be it status, power, or money—often stands to lose the most. Unfortunately, a person's need for love, admiration, and connection may be so strong that he distorts the true picture. Instead of seeing clearly what is happening, he remains naïve and oblivious of the self-serving motives of others and the realization that a breach of trust has taken place.

For all these reasons, friendship with a narcissist is fraught with problems. Though a narcissist's feelings for others may appear genuine, they are, in truth, shallow and laced with envy, contempt, or rage. A narcissist wants to be your friend or lover only if there's something in it for him. For all your efforts, you may be rewarded with anger and emotional coldness. After all, Admirers really aren't interested in you. They're interested in what you can do for them.

THEY JUST DON'T GET IT

As we saw with Rivals, an Admirer's betrayal can be especially hard to pinpoint in the workplace, since it's often unclear where the personal relationship ends and the professional one begins. Admirers exploit these hazy boundaries and believe that friendship gives them license to take advantage of you in a business setting. As one attorney told me, "My friends never pay me. You'd think that a friend would be respectful of my livelihood and would understand that when I look over a contract or file papers on his behalf, it takes time and I need to be reimbursed. But my invoice will sit on his desk for months, and I have to remind him several times to pay it. It's embarrassing; it makes me nuts; and it puts a real strain on the friendship." When friends behaved in self-serving ways, this man was confused and upset. On the other hand, had he been dealing strictly with business colleagues, he wouldn't have reacted this way. He would simply have had his accountant call and request payment.

Candace, who owned a graphic arts design company, had a similar, though far more hurtful, experience of friendship colliding with business goals. Candace hired Ruth, a bright and engaging woman with two school-age children, to be her assistant, and the two women formed an instant bond. Technically, Ruth was working for Candace, but the two were much more best buddies than boss and employee.

"Ruth was desperate to get back to work, now that her kids were older," Candace explained. "She didn't really have any skills, but I gave her a break. And I thought my instincts were on target; she not only turned out to be a hard worker, she was terrific fun to be with. I taught her everything I knew. But I thought she was there for me, too," Candace continued. "When my mother had a heart attack and was hovering near death for weeks, I saw Ruth as my rock. I counted on her to run the office and to be a support through the whole ordeal."

Needless to say, Candace was shocked when, without warning, Ruth announced she was opening a competing agency. While Candace had been preoccupied with her mother's illness, she had no idea that Ruth was quietly stealing her client list by offering everyone better deals. Though shaken by the news, Candace was unable to confront her friend, remaining distant but still hoping to maintain a relationship with her. That is, until the night Ruth borrowed her favorite black jacket and returned it with a cigarette burn.

"That did it for me," Candace snapped. "All the little betrayals suddenly came into focus. I realized I was the one literally getting burned in this relationship. I hated her, and hated myself for having put up with her for so long."

Like other Admirers, Ruth had violated one boundary after another, although Candace had been unaware and unable to see it. Nevertheless, Ruth felt her conscience was clear. As far as she was concerned, she'd been doing all the nitty-gritty work, dealing with client problems on a daily basis, so why shouldn't she ask them to join her new agency? What's more, like many narcissistic people, Ruth became indignant when Candace confronted her.

It's important to keep in mind that, while the Admirer's breach of trust may appear to be the same as that of the User, whom we'll meet in the next chapter, her betrayals are not as deliberate or as calculating. Kimberly, Sophia, and Ruth, for example, simply didn't care about the effect of their actions. Their grandiose sense of themselves led them to believe that they truly were entitled to what they took. They acted as if their ideas were original. This by-product of narcissism is what made them so untrustworthy.

Even when a person realizes that he has been deceived by an Admirer, he may be so caught up in the relationship that he is unable to extricate himself. During her last year in graduate school, Audrey was involved in such a relationship with Graham, a fellow student. "He was my studymate and my best friend," Audrey explained. "We could talk about anything and everything; he never failed to tell me how bright and articulate I was, and that he wished he could present his views as cogently as I did mine."

When Audrey decided to run for student body president, Graham was the one she told first. "He was my biggest supporter," she recalled, still dazed from the shock of learning that her trusted friend had also placed his own name in nomination. "When I asked him why he did it, he looked surprised that I would question his actions. He told me that if I wanted him to withdraw, he would—and I found myself saying, 'Oh, no, don't do that.' Instead, I even came up with another idea, that we run as a dual candidacy," she told me.

It wasn't until much later that Audrey realized she had shot herself in the foot. "I didn't want to run as a co-president. I wanted to be president. Why did I get myself into such a mess?" Yet she still tried to stay connected with Graham, despite his overt self-serving actions. It took another betrayal on Graham's part—this time, when Audrey suggested that they establish a new campus committee, Graham stole the idea and presented it to the dean as his own—before Audrey finally woke up. Confiscating another's ideas, painting them as his own, is a classic Admirer's ploy.

YOUR PERSONAL RISK FACTORS

As I noted, the subtle shifts of the admiring relationship gone awry can be difficult to spot. Many times, you may sense that something is wrong, but you can't put your finger on it. In fact, you may even feel silly, overly suspicious, or crass in thinking that someone you admire, and who clearly admires and supports you, could possibly undercut you. Not until a specific incident occurs—an obvious play for your job, a seat taken at a board meeting, a jacket returned in ruins—do you finally say, 'Wait a minute, I *am* being taken advantage of! I'm being had!'

Study the following risk factors; they may help you detect

early on at what point a seemingly trustworthy Admirer is overstepping the bounds.

Risk Factor #1:
You Need the Constant Admiration and Praise of Others to Feel Good About Yourself

You may not feel totally secure about your looks, your intelligence, or your abilities. Like Helen, you may have accomplished much, but lingering doubts of childhood remain and you still feel vulnerable. You need others to tell you how smart you are or how good you look to help you maintain positive feelings about yourself. You may not completely trust your judgment, either, so before you make a decision, large or small, you seek reassurance and approval from others. Because your self-esteem is tied to the constant support or admiration of others, your need may blind you to their self-serving actions.

Risk Factor #2:
You're a People Pleaser

You're the kind of person who can't say no. You feel obligated to help others, guilt-ridden when you don't. For you, as for Candace, saying yes—doing for and giving to others—makes you feel good, important, and needed. In fact, without the esteem of others, you may feel hollow, useless, and worthless. You feel powerful that you have valuable resources and contacts, which you can use to help the person who admires you and whom you admire. As a result, you may use these resources generously, giving of your money, time, energy, and attention. The recipient of your largesse is always appreciative and tells you over and over that he could never manage without you. Being indispensable to another becomes a vital ingredient of your self-esteem.

The problem is, you are only as good as the last thing you have done. When he gets angry and discounts your efforts, you are apt to try even harder to regain his approval. Consequently, you don't even realize when your energy is being depleted. You may be astonished, in fact, at how easily he asks you to do the most burdensome things, and that never stops you from accommodating his brazen requests.

Risk Factor #3: You Seek Out Others to Make Yourself Feel Whole

You look to blend your world with someone else's. By forming this power pact, so to speak, you believe you are strengthening your status and identity. You see this power pact as something from which you stand to gain. As Sophia did for Myra, the Admirer may provide you with a missing piece of your personality and lifestyle. Perhaps she offers you the family you never had, or the opportunity to share in experiences you always yearned for but never had the chance to participate in. The fact that she accepts you and draws you into her life is a stamp of approval. You must have what it takes, after all.

FIVE WAYS TO SPOT ADMIRERS

1. They constantly tell you you're the best and wish they could be just like you. "You're so smart. Why do things come so easy for you?" is a common refrain.

2. They imitate your style—do what you do, where you go, and dress the way you do, often without asking permission or inquiring whether or not you care. Did you join the new health club? They sign up, too. Did you buy that suit at the boutique in town? They'll go out and buy the same one.

3. Since they convince you that they can't survive without you, you go overboard in doing for, and giving to, them. They promise to do you a favor, but never deliver unless it's convenient for them.

4. They exude a sense of entitlement. Go out of your way for them, and they act as if they expected nothing less.

5. They forget yesterday, and remember only what you're doing for them today.

QUICK TIPS:
HOW TO OUTSMART ADMIRERS

1. Don't overextend yourself. Learn to say no. For more on setting limits, see Chapter 10.
2. Guard the personal information you share as well as whom you share it with.
3. Change your expectations. Broaden your social network so that you rely less on Admirers to meet your need for self-esteem.
4. Learn to confront Admirers when necessary to protect yourself from their violating behaviors. Check out the Confrontation Strategy in Chapter 8.
5. Realize and remember: something is wrong with their perspective, not with you. Therefore, no matter how much you do for Admirers, in their eyes, it will never be enough.

Now it's time to take a look at Users, the most insidious betrayers of trust. Like Admirers, Users also possess a sense of entitlement. But more than that, they completely distort reality and live exclusively by the principle that the ends justify the means. Users deny any wrongdoing or responsibility for their deceptions and, not surprisingly, this obstinacy becomes the driving force that fuels the victims' need for retaliation.

CHAPTER 6

Users: *"Winner Takes All"*

Victor, a handsome real estate broker, was never at a loss for female companionship, which is why Marilyn, a stunning redhead who is personnel director for a large hospital, was surprised and thrilled when he asked her out. After three months of serious dating, Victor moved into Marilyn's apartment, promising that they'd be married "sometime soon." Meanwhile, Marilyn, who had just celebrated her fortieth birthday, supported them, since Victor never seemed to have any money, despite his full-time job. It didn't matter, Marilyn told herself. It was worth it just to have someone like Victor in her life, so much so that she was willing to lend him $18,000 for a business investment.

But as the months passed, Marilyn found it harder and harder to rationalize Victor's behavior. When they went out, he'd invariably keep her waiting at a restaurant for an hour. Knowing she was insecure about her looks—as a child, she'd been seriously overweight—he'd make critical comments about her appearance, often in a backhanded way. "Why don't you wear a dress like Rita's?" he'd ask. Even his praise hid subtle putdowns, and no matter what she did, Marilyn never felt pretty enough or talented enough. The night she came home thrilled with a new haircut, Victor said, "Your hair looked better the other way. Why'd you change it?"

Particularly upsetting was the way he thought nothing of inviting women friends to join them for dinner or brunch on the weekend without checking with her first. "He'd tell me So-and-So was joining us—that she was a potential client—and he'd wind up flirting with her the whole meal," she reported. "If I told him his behavior made me uncomfortable, he'd look at me as if I was nuts and say, 'How can you be like that? I need to socialize to make these connections. This is business!' Maybe it was," Marilyn added, "but it upset me a lot."

Indeed, Victor lived his life with Marilyn as if he were single, accounting for neither his time nor his whereabouts. Like all Users, he deliberately misled her, promising marriage and talking often about their future together. Comforted to some extent in knowing that he was financially indebted to her, Marilyn tried hard not to be overly sensitive; several past relationships had crumbled for just that reason. "I have quite a temper when I get going," she said with a sigh, "and I didn't want to blow it."

But time and again, pushed to the edge, she did blow up. That's when Victor, a master political spin doctor, would glare incredulously. "What's wrong with you? Look at how you're acting . . . you're such a bitch," he'd say, slowly and evenly. "You want to know why we're not getting along . . . why I'm not sure I want to stay with you? Because you always make such a big deal out of nothing. You're totally inflexible and completely out of control!"

What's more, he'd add, she was the one with the problem. "And if you don't like it, you can just leave." The one time she did walk out, Victor transformed himself into the kind, reassuring, and sensitive man she had fallen in love with.

Turning the problem inside out, flipping the blame back to the victim, are classic maneuvers of a User like Victor. After all, at those moments, Marilyn was out of control. It's understandable that she began to doubt herself and think, "He's right. I am a bitch . . . it is my fault." Marilyn didn't see that Victor had set her up for repeated breaches of trust. He kept her hooked by pouring on the flattery and charm—albeit inconsistently and in small doses, and always after he had already chipped away at her self-esteem. Victor's praise, like the praise of every User, was repair work, something he'd throw her way after he'd broken her down.

However, because Marilyn so desperately needed this emotional affirmation, she, like other victims, felt compelled to keep the relationship alive, and dreaded the day she'd make Victor so angry that he'd leave for good. She'd been warned about Victor. Both his mother and his ex-wife, whom Marilyn often encountered when Victor picked up his children for weekend visits, had recounted tales of his unreliability and outright hurtfulness. Marilyn listened, but didn't hear. She truly believed she'd be the one to change him, the one person he would treat differently from everyone else.

We meet Users like Victor everywhere; they make regular appearances in romantic or workplace situations. The User may be the man in your life who insists you're the most sensational woman he's ever met, who promises you tomorrow but isn't around today. She may be the friend who desperately needs $500 to pay a credit-card bill, but never once mentions paying you back. Or perhaps he's the colleague who convinces you to tap your best connections to close an important deal, then cuts you out at the last minute. We even meet Users within families, when marital partners profess love with one eye on the bank account, when siblings who are business partners proclaim loyalty but then siphon off profits for themselves, or when adult children bilk aged parents or relatives out of their life savings. Abuse of the elderly, experts report, is a growing national scandal.

Users betray not just by what they do, but in what they promise and then deliberately fail to do. Users will stop at nothing to engender sympathy so that others will support them and help them achieve their goals. They don't indulge in petty games of one-upmanship, the way Rivals do. And while they come on strong and are focused exclusively on their own needs, Users, like Admirers, take self-absorption to another level. Guilt is not in their vocabulary. Exploitation is.

THE WAY THEY DO THE THINGS
THEY DO

Victor, for example, knew Marilyn was insecure about her appearance, so he regularly, and purposely, pushed her hot buttons. "That dress doesn't look so great," he'd say as they were on their way to a black-tie charity dinner. "Did you gain a few pounds?" Indeed, a User knows his victim's Achilles' heel well—and goes for it. Like the husband in *Gaslight,* the classic 1944 movie starring Ingrid Bergman and Charles Boyer, in which the husband schemed to make his wife think she was crazy, Users betray a trust by twisting reality so that victims believe they are to blame for the problems they face. Each time Marilyn was forced to endure yet another emotional assault, the experience confirmed her secret fear that there really was something wrong with her. After all, who in their right mind would put up with such a hurtful man?

What's more, no matter how unbearable the situation, the target of a User believes she has no choice but to remain, because no one else will want her or do as much for her. In fact, the cycle of psychological dependency that Users establish is akin to what we see in verbally and physically abusive relationships. In both cases, victims are unable to leave because they see no way out.

As Users play on a victim's dependency, they continue their detective work, unearthing a victim's needs, priorities, values, and goals, and then, chameleonlike, changing themselves to match that image. Users tell the victim what she wants to hear and impress her with how much he can do for her. They evoke trust in words but breach it with actions. In fact, while the dichotomy between what one says and what one does is present whenever trust is broken, in the case of a User it stands out in sharp relief. With bursts of bravado, a User will seduce, hustle, and deceive, employing whatever it takes to convince a victim how much happier or successful her life will be with him. A User's charm is his lifeline.

When Denise was setting up her new company to publish a fashion industry newsletter, she was introduced to Gordon, an executive at a publishing company who was looking for a business partner. Over many lunches and afterwork drinks, the two got to know each other and realized that their goals, abilities, and experience were a good match. "I was really excited about working with Gordon," Denise says. "We were very much in sync. I remember telling him that, for me, the number one quality in a partner is follow-through, which seemed to fit Gordon to a T. He said he'd call me on Thursday to follow up on our plans, and he did. When he said he'd look into the price of office space, he had three real estate brokers lined up to search for us. Small details like that impressed me. I never had to ask twice."

Indeed, Denise was working such long hours that it took several months for her to realize that Gordon had stopped following through. Like many people in the clutches of a User, she brushed aside any percolating feelings of doubt. It was just a coincidence, she said, that a particular deal Gordon had told her was "in the bag" fell through. He had reasonable excuses for others that "didn't work out," yet continued to offer Denise the reassurance and encouragement that, together, they'd be a bigger success than she'd ever dreamed—another typical User ploy. She even dismissed Gordon's disparaging remarks about deals she brought in independently. Many people are so focused on their goal—Marilyn on marrying and raising a family; Denise on being successful at work—that they don't see the inconsistencies in a User's behavior. "Gordon rented expensive office space, took the largest office on the floor, but failed to bring in one advertising account," Denise recalled. "And like a fool, I didn't add it all up."

What's more, as we saw with Marilyn, if someone else dares to point out how much a User is taking advantage of them, victims invariably rise to their defense: "My husband told me outright, 'I don't trust him,' " Denise later admitted. "I actually got pissed off at him."

Gordon is a partner vulture, a User who feeds off the creativity of others, devouring their ideas before moving on to other prey. After almost a year, Denise understood what was happening and severed the relationship. She wasn't the first nor the last to be used by Gordon. A colleague recently reported that he had found another victim and was going into partnership with him.

Marilyn and Denise learned the hard way. Despite the warnings of others, victims of Users are like Dorothy in *The Wizard of Oz*, who didn't realize until the end of the movie that she could go home to Kansas by simply clicking her red-slippered heels together twice. Like Dorothy, they struggle and endure great emotional turmoil before they are able to see clearly that they have the power within themselves to change the patterns of their interactions and take control of their lives.

It's not uncommon for people to have a history of involvement with one User after another. Users give just enough to keep people hooked and dependent; and so, like heroin addicts, targets of betrayal feel so inherently insecure, and are so dependent on Users' resources that they keep coming back for more.

Paula, a successful commercial photographer in Seattle, had such a history. A child of an overbearing, critical father, she married right out of art school to escape an unhappy home life. Her ten-year marriage—to a man who had used all her contacts to get his own career off the ground—fell apart. When he left her after he became successful, she was desperate to pull her life together. One step in the right direction, she reasoned, was to sign with Ryan, a well-known agent who had been wooing her for years with promises of high-paying jobs in television and film.

Proud of her decision, Paula didn't realize that Ryan, with Machiavellian maneuvers, had begun to undermine her career, lying about contacting studios on her behalf and even pitching her ideas as the work of other clients. At first, she chalked up the losses to coincidence. Whenever she did muster the courage to confront him, "he'd blow up and I'd always back down," Paula said. "I'd wind up apologizing and feeling guilty for doubting him in the first place. Somehow, he'd always convince me that he was the only one who could set my career on fire." Paula knew, on some level, that her relationship with Ryan was toxic, but she couldn't break it. To be treated so shabbily felt emotionally familiar: it was the way both her father and her husband had treated her.

Inevitably, Users like Ryan deny any wrongdoing or responsibility for their actions. Boiling with self-righteous indignation and self-importance, they make you feel ungrateful and guilty that you could for one minute doubt their motives. They really have your best interests at heart, they point out over and over—why can't you see that? "Look at how much

I've done for you!" a User will exclaim. "I didn't do this for me; I did it for you!"

But of course Users have their own interests at heart. No matter how much you try to convince a User of your point of view, he cannot see it. As a result, every time you interact with such a betrayer, you feel stupid. Though you know better, you constantly leave yourself vulnerable to breaches of trust, and despite your best efforts, you can't protect yourself. If you dare to question a User, he, like Victor, Gordon, or Ryan, will give you only pieces of the truth, which never add up. Confront him further, and he foams with rage or freezes you out of his life. But since you're hooked, once the thaw is over you're so grateful and relieved that you simply ignore what preceded it. However, the moment you no longer have anything to offer a User, he will dismiss you from his life.

Another reason Users are successful is that so many people subscribe to the Trust Factor discussed in Chapter 1: that no one is perfect and you have to accept the good with the bad. Especially in romance, many women rise to the challenge of taming an incorrigible man. They want to think that they can change a wayward guy and put him on track. Mistaking lust for love and trust, they are easily duped by those who have no compunction about lying or cheating to achieve their goals. The excitement, even the danger, of the quest makes a User attractive.

"He was a con man, no doubt about it," one woman told me. "I knew about his love-'em-and-leave-'em reputation. But it didn't matter. What a fool I was . . . I actually thought I was so special, I'd be the one to get him to change." In truth, whenever you are involved with a User, you are always the loser.

WHY THEY DO THE THINGS
THEY DO

What kind of person exploits others this way? Users run the gamut from people like Victor and Ryan to, in the most extreme cases, the con artists, bigamists, and thieves who rob their victims of love, emotional support, and financial resources.

Take the case of Margaret, a fifty-one-year-old former guidance counselor and the mother of two college-age children. She had recently been widowed, after twenty-one years of marriage; then, through a dating service, Margaret met and fell in love with fifty-two-year-old Howard, the charming divorced father of three and a principal owner of a large personnel agency. After dating for one year, they were married—and little by little, Margaret began to doubt whether her Prince Charming was for real.

There were little inconsistencies that cropped up from time to time—lapses in memory, the fact that he changed jobs several times, that he had lied about his age. "When I discovered that he was really fifty-nine—I had to look for something in his dresser, and I found an old driver's license—he said he'd lied because he loved me too much to lose me," she says. "He insisted I was the love of his life and thought I wouldn't want to marry such an old man."

But when Howard went to visit his mother for an extended vacation, and refused to allow her to join him, Margaret began to suspect her husband wasn't the man she thought he was. After hiring a private detective, she learned that

Howard had been married twice before—and still was married. "I should have checked, but I didn't. These con men are very good liars. And perhaps I wanted to believe what he was saying. I wanted to trust him."

The newspapers are filled with stories of people like Margaret, lonely, sad, lost souls who are so easily duped by charming lovers that they fail to discover—or, even worse, blatantly ignore—a User's numerous identities or infidelities. Many times, these people are so emotionally broken themselves, they're unable to trust their own judgment, even when confronted with the hard evidence. But the truth is, Users have tremendous difficulty sustaining warm, close relationships. Afraid of intimacy, threatened by being close, they protect themselves by never letting down their guard. To them, closeness feels like entrapment and control. Instead of getting involved, they get what they want.

Of course, men aren't the only con artists. Women scam men. Forty-four-year-old Bernice, for example, has been married and divorced twice and has a ten-year-old daughter. Though not especially pretty, Bernice has a terrific body—and uses it to attract one man after another. Bernice has been engaged to Alan, a workaholic businessman, for four years, and she demands that he pay for all her clothes and jewelry as well as her hair styling and manicure twice a week.

However, her engagement hasn't stopped her from seeing others. On the nights she entertains other men, Bernice tells Alan to sleep at his mother's house, since, she says, she's going to dinner with some girlfriends. For the last five months, she's been dating Arthur, a construction contractor who has been home for six months on disability leave from work. Arthur knows nothing about Alan, and has told Bernice he'd do anything for her—and does. He runs her errands, shops for groceries, cleans the house while she's out, and even picks up her daughter after school. Meanwhile, Bernice cashes Arthur's disability checks, uses the money to cover those expenses not covered by Alan, and doles out the rest to Arthur.

As we saw in the preceding chapter, narcissists have little capacity for empathy. However, Users like Bernice have no empathy at all. They don't care how their behavior affects others. Indeed, Users may have a history of antisocial behavior, often triggered by some childhood trauma, such as a bitter parental divorce, physical or verbal abuse, or lack of love and nurturing from their critical or punitive parents. They grow up angry, believing the world owes them and that others will pay for what they've been through. Users have no trouble breaking the rules to suit their needs. They believe their having been wronged gives them leave to hurt someone else.

Victor's father, for example, died when Victor was seven, and his mother was rarely around. When she was, she was controlling and often verbally abusive to her son. Victor became the class bully, and by the time he was in junior high school, he'd been picked up by the police for breaking car windows and shoplifting. Victor dealt with the pain of his father's early death and his mother's rejection by directing his anger outward and hurting everyone else. In fact, Users, even more than Admirers, believe they're entitled to do whatever they want. They've been cheated, so they feel little guilt when they cheat others.

Not surprisingly, Users often have difficulty holding a job. They change positions frequently or get fired, but externalize all the blame. It's never because of any incompetence on their part, but, rather, "because everyone else has an attitude," or "the boss is out to get me." They are never responsible for their current situation or predicament. Typically, Users fail to honor financial obligations, whether it's paying back a loan or paying child support; again, they insist it's through no fault of their own. Users employ every excuse in the book to let themselves off the hook.

YOUR PERSONAL RISK FACTORS

When Users are challenged, their rage may be explosive. Their best defense is a good offense. Contrary to his public persona, a User's ego is quite fragile. Being close makes a User feel vulnerable, helpless, humiliated. Needing anyone else seems to him a sign of weakness, so he avoids intimacy at all costs. Preying on others is the only way he can emotionally feed himself. His charm is his survival skill—that's why he is so good at using it. He believes no one can stop him, and because he is so quick to violate a trust, he *is* hard to stop.

Still, though we can paint a fairly complete picture of the User, he can be extraordinarily difficult to recognize when he is scamming you, and that makes it even more difficult for you to break free. The first step is to realize that you are vulnerable to the User's betrayal of trust. Do any of the following Risk Factors feel familiar?

Risk Factor #1:
Secretly, You Feel Inadequate

Do you feel, deep down, that there really is something wrong with you . . . that you're lacking an essential quality? Do you often find yourself saying, "I'm so stupid, I'm fat, I'm selfish, I'm lazy"? On the surface, you may seem to others strong and secure, bright and talented. Only you know that you're unable to hold on to those feelings, because a core of self-doubt always kicks in. Childhood hurts lie buried close to the surface. Perhaps you were overweight, like Marilyn, or painfully shy, and it doesn't take much to trigger the old anxiety. More often than you care to admit, you feel alone, often lonely. Giving someone a chance to prove his love to you makes you feel lovable and affirms your self-worth.

Risk Factor #2:
You Are at a Vulnerable Time in Your Life

Have you recently been divorced or lost a spouse? Are you a woman in her late thirties whose biological clock is ticking loudly and you are afraid you may never find a mate, let alone raise a family? Perhaps you recently ended a bad relationship, and now feel empty and fragile. Then, too, you may be entering a stage in your life—perhaps celebrating a landmark birthday—when you take stock of your accomplishments, find yourself wanting, and reach out blindly to anyone who professes love. Fueled by a sense of urgency, even desperation, you become involved with someone who reinforces your old insecurities and personal doubts. As Margaret finally admitted, "I couldn't see the warning signs, though they were all around me. I didn't know what to look for."

Risk Factor #3:
You Often Wonder, Is It Him or Is It Me?

Are you ambivalent about the person with whom you're involved? Do you love him one day, hate him the next? Do you question his motives? Someone who is vulnerable to a User is often confused and unsure of how she thinks or feels. Rather than trust her own judgment, she solicits another's opinions. However, in time, seemingly trusted advice begins to feel like controlling orders. In fact, any challenge on your part makes the other person angry and defensive. As we noted in the chapter on blind trust, you may be in Trust Sandtrap #2—insisting that you are merely giving a person a chance to prove his trust, and denying that he could possibly be so calculating.

You also may be stuck in Sandtrap #3—feeling that you have to accept the good with the bad. He keeps you hooked by flooding you with apologies and promises to change, swearing his devotion, and pleading despair at the prospect of life without you. His calculated pull is so strong, you probably believe you're too demanding and are a terrible person if you don't accept him with all his faults and love him for who he is. As a result, you may miss or misinterpret vital information that would help you reframe the relationship. You experience betrayal, but you let it go, pretending it never happened or will never happen again.

Risk Factor #4:
You Mistake Lust for Love

Did you recently end a passionless relationship, in which you either felt undesired or were sexually turned off? Your sexual self-esteem may have been clobbered, and as a result, when you enter another relationship where the sexual chemistry is potent, you are easily hooked. A User is a master at the art of seduction, and you finally feel you are attractive and desirable. The challenge, danger, and excitement of the relationship attract you and blind you to potential land mines. Rather than ask yourself whether this person is kind, honest, loyal, dependable, supportive, and trustworthy, you can think only that the sex is great, so the relationship must be, too. You reason: she really desires me; she must love me; the relationship has to work.

Risk Factor #5:
You're a Superhelper

Do you feel guilty and selfish when asserting your needs? Does asking for what you want make you feel like a User yourself? More than simply wanting to please others, do you go overboard in your efforts to help? People at risk for domination by a User don't have a clear sense of what they can expect of others in a close relationship. In fact, whenever they do make a request of another, they fear they're being greedy, demanding, and overstepping their bounds. You may keep giving, despite the fact that you are emotionally and physically depleted.

Even though you get little in return, you continue to give, fueled by the belief that in time you will get something back. Like Marilyn, you may need to exert control, however tenuous, by making the other person dependent on you financially. Desperate to be loved, you may tie your self-esteem to your efforts to make the other person's life better at the expense of your own.

SIX WAYS TO UNCOVER A USER

1. What Users say and what they do are miles apart. They tell you what you want to hear, but they never follow through.
2. Users undermine your self-confidence and make you feel dependent on them by building you up and then cutting you down. "You're the prettiest woman in the room," he croons, "but why didn't you wear the red dress? You look much sexier in it."
3. Users never give you an honest answer: they lie outright, proffer half-truths, or pass the blame. The bottom line: the pieces of the puzzle never fit together.
4. Users make you feel guilty—and that there's something wrong with you—if you doubt them or question their intentions.
5. Users make you feel greedy or selfish for asserting your needs.
6. Users react angrily if you confront them, perhaps by storming off, shutting down, or flipping the situation around and blaming you.

QUICK TIPS:
USURPING A USER

1. Build up your self-esteem so that you have the inner strength to trust your instincts. See Chapter 10.
2. Don't dismiss actions or words if you sense something's amiss. Trust a person's words only when his behavior is consistent with what he says. It's not just what he says; it's what he does.
3. Keep a record of what occurs and how you feel so that you can track patterns of behavior. Refer to this record when you have the courage to initiate a confrontation with a User. See Chapter 8 for suggestions on doing this.
4. Learn to set limits for yourself when dealing with a User's anger. In Chapter 10, you'll learn how to do that.

SECTION III

The Fallout from Betrayal

CHAPTER 7

Revenge: "I'll Make You Pay"

The bully of a boss who demands your time and dedication but fails to give you the raise you deserve . . .

The lover who year after year promises to divorce his wife but never does . . .

The boyfriend who insists he's just not the marrying kind, then ditches you to wed another.

Stories that prompt revenge, that push people to the edge, and over it, are legion. They are the stuff of Greek myths, Shakespearean plays—and today's sordid newspaper headlines.

Yet who hasn't indulged in a revenge fantasy of one kind or another, or vowed to get even with the person "who done you wrong?" When trust is broken, it's human nature to want to retaliate in some way. In fact, the fantasy for retribution, to make the other person pay for the way he or she has hurt you, can sometimes be gut-wrenchingly cathartic. Audiences love watching celluloid heroes like Sylvester Stallone and Arnold Schwarzenegger zap their enemies and withstand whizzing bullets as they right the wrongs and make the bad guys pay for their dastardly deeds. The emotional release makes us feel more powerful, more in control of our lives.

Revenge, at least on the silver screen, seems like a good thing. Is it? Outside the darkened theater, the line between what you should and shouldn't do in the wake of betrayal is not so precisely drawn. In real life, the act of revenge often harms the revenger far more than the target. As you'll see in this chapter, revenge is not always sweet; and there are far more effective—and healthy—ways to deal with broken trust.

SETTLING THE SCORE

What drives people to seek revenge? Sometimes revenge is simply the immature reaction to a perceived slight or behavior that you consider hostile or offensive. Lucy, driving to town on an errand, was waiting patiently for a parking space when another driver zipped around her and slid into the space. Livid, Lucy took her keys and carved a long, wavy scratch in the side of his car. Phyllis was so offended by a surly waiter who made her feel she wasn't good enough to eat in his fancy restaurant that she left a penny for a tip.

In these cases, people seek to assuage their damaged dignity. With their egos on the line, it becomes imperative for them to do something—however petty—to remedy the wrong. The offenses may well be wholly imagined; still, in their minds, the behavior had malicious motives; someone was deliberately out to get them.

On a larger scale, when a true betrayal occurs, revenge is the means by which people search to protect themselves from further injustice and prove their strength. They feel cut down and put down, and their world spins out of control. Revenge seems the only way to even the score and regain a sense of stability.

The impulse to strike back is a primitive response; every animal fights back when attacked. The Bible calls for an eye for an eye—a victim should never rest until he exacted revenge in kind from his enemy. And while most of us were weaned on the virtue of "turning the other cheek," the need to retaliate against someone who has cheated or betrayed us is deeply ingrained.

Retaliation is also a way to deal with rejection and to rebuild self-esteem. Our hitting back, some of us reason, will give betrayers a taste of their own medicine and makes them feel as bad as we do—maybe even worse. Many people believe that the only means by which they can convey their suffering is by turning the ordeal into their betrayer's ordeal as well. Then the perpetrator will understand the pain he caused. Only then will the victim feel redeemed. The feeling of being wronged is so engulfing that one's whole existence can revolve around the quest for justice.

As I noted in Chapter 2, a person's failure to be there for you when you fully expect him to be can also trigger the wish for revenge, and in some cases it can take decidedly hostile forms. A few months ago, the newspapers reported in lurid detail the tale of a well-known romance novelist, who, feeling abandoned and betrayed by a long-time friend, participated in a scheme to break into his apartment and steal over $800,000 worth of art and antiques. Why did she do it? Because, she told police, when she had cried to him about her despair over the death of her mother, the breakup with her lover, and her desire to kill herself, he had flippantly responded, "Well, do what you have to do." Granted, this man's response was surely not understanding or supportive. Whether he meant it in jest or was, in fact, fed up with her demands and laments, she experienced it as a profound abandonment, one that was so excruciating, it could be soothed only by an equally harsh act of revenge.

In some cases, revenge is also a defense against unbearable sadness, humiliation, and shame. If a colleague promises to support you at an important meeting and then doesn't speak up; if a spouse has an affair; if parents insist you've wasted your life and are a disappointment to them, you feel ridiculed and exposed and aggrieved. Revenge is the way to save face and restore a sense of self-dignity. A slew of tell-all books bear witness to countless lost souls who have to speak out at the perceived wrongs of uncaring, neglectful parents, lovers, and even employers, who, they feel, let them down.

Everyone, from celebrities, presidents, and their first ladies to the British royal family, has been the target of I'll-get-even books. Remember *Mommie Dearest?* The books written by the children of Bette Davis, Bing Crosby, the Reagans—even Prince Charles's former butler—were all prompted by revenge. While the money earned from their publishing ventures helped to soothe these hurt souls, and was justified, they rationalized, by the misery long endured—the initial motive was most likely pure revenge, a desire to strike back and subject their betrayer to the same embarrassment and shame that their behavior initially caused. Judging from the runaway sales of such books, plenty of ordinary people can identify with those who bear grudges and are convinced that someone betrayed them in a fundamental way.

Revenge is sometimes plotted on a conscious and deliberate level. When Lynn's boss piled yet another major assignment on her desk, asking her to draft a proposal for a new building project yet did not give her the long-overdue raise she had promised many times, Lynn, an urban planner, knew she had reached her limit. Though she loved her job with this top engineering firm, and the work it involved, her boss was abusive and impossible to work for. Vowing to look for a new position, she rewrote her résumé and began to send out letters. Meanwhile, she slowed down the work she did at the office, and by making one excuse after another, each perfectly reasonable at the time, never got around to drafting that proposal. She also used her position and the entrée it gave her to make professional contacts, meet people for lunch—paid for by the company—and further her job search.

"Okay, so it wasn't the most ethical thing to do," Lynn admitted, "but I couldn't take it any more. My boss had taken advantage of me for eight years. I'd been loyal and gone beyond what my job called for, yet praise from her was rare—and any monetary acknowledgment of my hard efforts was nonexistent. I felt justified. I really made her pay in the end."

Whereas Lynn intentionally set out to get even, Gary's revenge was an unconscious act. Gary and Jeannie had dated for two years before becoming engaged during their final year in graduate school. But one month after graduation, Jeannie, pressured by her family, broke the engagement. For the next year, Gary rarely dated and dreamed constantly of being with Jeannie. When she finally called and said she was ready to resume the relationship, Gary took her back.

"How could I not?" Gary asked, rhetorically. "All I did was think about her for a solid year." But for Gary, the old passion and excitement never returned. Jeannie, however, started to make wedding plans—at which point Gary began an affair with a married woman.

"My relationship with this woman didn't mean anything," Gary insisted. "Jeannie found out when she heard a message from her on my answering machine. I knew the message was there, and actually thought about running upstairs and deleting it—but I didn't. It was stupid," he added. "The last thing I ever wanted to do was hurt Jeannie." Yet that's precisely what he did. Gary's omission and his affair were his unconscious revenge for past hurts. He had leveled the playing field.

Revenge flourishes in the marital arena, especially after a bitter separation or divorce. Sally, a homemaker, and Drew, a free-lance editor, were together for five years and had a four-year-old son, but the marriage came to an end when Drew fell in love with Meryl, Sally's best friend. Shattered, Sally embarked on a crusade she barely understood herself. She made harassing late-night phone calls to Drew's new apartment. She took out loans in her ex-husband's name; befriended his neighbors so that she could spy on him; and frequently came by his home when Meryl was at work. Saddest of all was the way she used her son as a pawn in her game of revenge, coaching him to tell Drew, "I hate Meryl and I want you and Mommy to get back together."

When infidelity occurs in a marriage, it's not uncommon for revenge to take the form of a tit-for-tat affair. Monica and

Carl are a case in point. Married for two years, these bright twentysomethings seemed the perfect couple. But Carl's one-night stand on a business trip led to a series of retaliatory affairs that eventually destroyed the marriage. When Monica discovered that Carl had slept with a colleague, she began an affair with a colleague of her own. Carl found out when the man called the house late one night and he picked up the phone. Furious, he launched into a two-hour tirade about how Monica had betrayed him and he could never trust her again, completely and conveniently ignoring that it was his initial betrayal of trust that had precipitated the crisis. Still, Monica continued to sleep with her co-worker. The revenge affair became her way of protecting herself from future betrayals—an action that virtually prevented them from ever adequately addressing and resolving what was wrong in their marriage, let alone rebuilding the trust necessary for a happy, healthy relationship.

Monica and Carl each was justified in feeling wronged, but instead of learning how to talk about their breach of trust, they, like many others who have suffered the pain of betrayal, ricocheted from one attack to another, each more wounding than the next. Every conversation disintegrated into a battle of blame as they fired shot after shot. Such an escalation of retaliation, the piling up of injustice on injustice, can develop into the consuming rage that may become a prelude to violence.

At its most extreme, getting even takes on a life of its own. Somehow, victims reason, if they can chip away at a betrayer's ego, or destroy his life, they will build back some of their own. Victims like Sally, for instance, can tap into no other resources than the persecution of the betrayer. They think they can fortify themselves by ruining the betrayer's new relationship, new marriage, or new job. Sally is unable to see that she cannot build herself up by tearing down someone else. Instead of finding a person who loves her as much as she loves him, she is wasting her energy obsessing about her ex-husband. What's more, she is betraying her son in her selfish game.

TACTICAL MANEUVERS

Revenge comes in many forms and is exacted on many levels as people plot emotional, social, financial, physical, and political ruin to avenge a wrong.

The most innocuous type of revenge is *wishful thinking*. In your mind, you're the great orator, never at a loss for words. You can stand up to the colleague who stole your ideas and presented them as her own, telling her what a conniving phony she is . . . telling a betraying lover what a self-serving, inconsiderate lowlife he is . . . letting a friend know, in no uncertain terms, that she's selfish and deceitful and you refuse to tolerate her sly machinations.

Of course, for most people, such on-target eloquence is nothing more than a fantasy. At times, it can provide a much-needed release from the frustration of dealing with broken trust and, to some extent, can help you process the pain. As you recite in your mind what you should have said or could have done, you feel cleansed and redeemed. Such vengeful fantasies serve their purpose and usually go no further.

At other times, people exact revenge by purposely doing nothing. This passive-aggressive behavior—provoking and infuriating someone by not doing what she asked you to do—is a common form of low-level revenge. If a friend reveals a secret you shared in confidence, you may "forget" to order the extra concert ticket she asked for. When a boyfriend flirts with your best friend at a party, you may refuse to have sex with him later that night. But such just-don't-do-it vengefulness can come back to haunt you.

Angie, an assistant in a public relations firm, was furious that her boss had refused her a raise, despite the long hours and many weekends of work she routinely did for him. For spite, she took far longer than necessary to type an important report she knew he needed for a strategic-planning meeting with his superior. Though Angie felt entirely justified at the time, it wasn't until later that she realized that sabotaging someone else often leads to self-sabotage. When her boss discovered that the report was late, he felt all the more entitled to withhold Angie's raise, and she lost any leverage she might have had in negotiating for it. The hard lesson Angie learned is that seeking revenge through avoidance can become your own undoing. By compromising her dignity and self-respect, she impaired her own performance and jeopardized her professional reputation.

Holding a *grudge* is another common form of revenge. A grudge is a sulky resentment that seems impossible to shed because it is your armor, protecting you from hurt while you work through the pain and begin to find the strength to move on. A grudge is the most frequent response to indirect malice, whether deliberate or perceived, such as lies, rumors, gossip, or character assaults. You can't prove, for instance, that your friend Jill was badmouthing you at work—in fact, the co-worker who told you about Jill's remarks may have made you promise not to say she told you—so you have nothing specific to confront her with. But you form a grudge, and stop talking to Jill.

In time, the heat of anger may subside and make room for

amends, for speaking with the person about your grievance and repairing the damage. In fact, holding a grudge can be useful if it is time-limited, and if you use it as a chance to re-evaluate your relationship and form a decision either to confront a betrayer of trust or to end the relationship. Jerry, whom we met in Chapter 4, held a grudge against Chris, his colleague who refused to give him a positive job reference, for about six weeks, refusing to take his phone calls or meet for their usual Friday night drinks. During that time, he took stock of his own feelings and figured out exactly what he wanted to do about the situation.

Needless to say, the longer you hold a grudge, the less opportunity you will have to understand what went wrong, why you were so gullible, and how you can be less vulnerable in the future. But when we don't have the words to express resentment or anger clearly, or simply don't want to, the pile of grievances mounts as we keep them to ourselves. Over time, built-up grudges become indistinguishable from one another until we find ourselves embroiled in a *cold war.* The objective here? To inflict deliberate pain and distress by rejecting the other person and severing the relationship.

In such cases, as in Chapter 4, with Jeff, who refused to forgive his brother Howard after he slept with his wife, Doreen—revenge is a retaliatory weapon that gives the victim a perverse sense of pleasure. Despite overtures on his brother's part, and entreaties from family members to patch things up, Jeff for several years refused to budge from his position. This refusal to forgive was his way of meting out punishment. Withdrawing his love was the only weapon he had left.

Cold wars can last a few days, a few months, or even years, bewildering the alleged betrayer, who may have only an inkling of your rage. In Chapter 3, we met Meredith and Beverly, two rising young stars in banking, whose friendship disintegrated after Beverly alleged that Meredith had betrayed her by blocking a job offer. Beverly didn't trust Meredith enough to know that she would not deliberately hurt her. In her anger, she refused all overtures and never gave Meredith a chance to explain why she had acted as she did. Instead, she made assumptions, carved them in stone, and refused to make amends. She should have checked out the complete situation, but since she didn't, she was left to live with her own version of it, and she became the victim of a cold war of her own making.

The silence of a cold war can be more devastating than any outpouring of anger. Cold warriors leave their targets to deal with confusion and guilt, and give them no chance to explain their motives or defend their actions. The anger is more important than either its cause or its potential solution. The consequence of such a cold war is that people like Beverly remain stuck. In punishing the one who let them down, they harbor a burning anger and run the risk of replicating the same pattern of interactions in other relationships.

At the far end of the revenge spectrum is *vindictiveness,* out-of-control rage directed at the one person you are convinced has caused your ruin, whose searing betrayal, you insist, provoked you to retaliate. This is the most self-destructive form of revenge—when taking revenge becomes an end unto itself—and you seek nothing less than vengeance.

People consumed with vindictiveness express no desire to confront a betrayer, to win him back, or to repair the relationship. Hateful feelings swamp them, and they feel little guilt, remorse, or responsibility for their behavior. What's more, an apology, if offered, may intensify their anger, because it validates their feelings and therefore justifies revenge. As we saw in Chapter 4, Melissa was so enraged when Carly "stole" her long-time boyfriend that she refused to accept her apologies. The more Carly tried to make amends, the more justified Melissa felt in striking back by making harrassing late-night phone calls to her home and even following her when she and Gary went out. In fact, vindictiveness taken to its extreme can lead to the stalking behavior reported in countless cases of domestic abuse or even the jealous rages that lead to murder.

Bonnie, twenty-four, a former cheerleader and star of the high school soccer team, had been trying to break up with Roy, her boyfriend of two years, for several months, but he refused to allow her to go. Possessive to the point of obsession, he followed her to work, hid in the bushes outside her house, and even called her repeatedly to curse her out, hanging up whenever someone else answered the phone. Unable to contain his fury, he marched into the diner where she worked as a waitress and, as co-workers and customers looked on in horror, shot her in the chest and then turned the gun on himself.

Such tales of horror fill the airwaves and newspapers. In these cases, it often appears to all the world that the vindictive person wants his partner back, but what he really wants is to get back at her. The consequences of his actions simply don't matter anymore. Since he already feels his life has lost its meaning, he irrationally and singlemindedly seeks either to end the alleged betrayer's life, or to render it as joyless as his own. To accomplish this goal, he targets the one thing the betrayer loves the most or makes her most vulnerable.

For instance, if the betrayer holds a position of power in the business world, his victim may try to undercut his professional status and tarnish his reputation. Jackie was heartbroken and furious when Sid, a young accountant, broke off their two-year relationship to date a supposedly close friend of hers, and she didn't see or speak to him for six months, until they ran into each other at a friend's party. But that night seemed like old times. "Sid was gentle, considerate, and funny," Jackie recalled, "and when he offered to drive me home, I figured it couldn't hurt to invite him in for a drink." But when Jackie excused herself to go to the bathroom, Sid got undressed and hopped into bed. Jackie was horrified. "How could he expect me to sleep with him?" she asked, her voice still shaking with anger several months later. Jackie was angry that Sid had assumed he could pick up their relationship where it had ended, and the evening quickly disintegrated into such a heated battle that neighbors called the police. When the officers knocked on her door, Jackie blurted out, "He tried to rape me!" Rage that had simmered under the surface for months exploded in that one accusation. Though unfounded, the accusation and ensuing publicity did not sit well with Sid's partners, who pressured him to resign from the firm.

Similarly, a betrayed spouse may use the children in a tug-of-war with a former wife or husband. In one gruesome scenario, the result was murder. Eric, an architect, was so enraged when Joyce, his wife of fifteen years, left him that he killed their eight-year-old son and then committed suicide. Eric believed his life was over; by killing his child he was also destroying part of himself. For people like Eric, the betrayal is so profound and the rage so blinding that they neither see nor care about the impact of their revenge.

Doug was similarly maddened when his ex-wife remarried and moved with their two children halfway across the country: "She can't take my kids away from me," he told me in one heated session. "I won't let her. I'll kill her first." Doug planned to run his ex-wife over with his car, and it was not easy getting him past his blind rage to see the effect his fury would have, not only on his life, but also on his children's. "They'll lose both parents," I pointed out. "Your wife will be dead, and you'll be in jail."

However, by expressing his vengeful fantasy, and verbalizing his anger with me, Doug eventually was able to calm down. Finally, he could see that if he followed through with his fantasy, he would lose everything that was important to him: his children and the business he had built from scratch.

The desire for revenge can lead you to think out loud, to share revenge fantasies, and to talk with those you do trust about how you were wronged. Such conversations are one part of the healthy healing process, in which you let go of past hurts and move on with courage and hope that your world can be restored and be safe once again.

However, when talking to others inflames your anger and provokes you to turn your fantasies into reality; when your rage hurts innocent people—for example, the wife who puts her son in the middle of her divorce battle, and forces him to wrestle with divided loyalties—or when your anger is far out of proportion to the perceived betrayal, revenge is self-destructive.

When my clients can't see beyond their anger, I often help them learn to manage it by explaining that anger is energy. It can fuel you if you harness it in a positive way, like a car that uses gas to run. But if you flood the engine, it stalls out. In much the same way, when you're flooded with vengeful feelings, you become immobilized and can't move forward. You remain emotionally stuck, tied by an all-consuming obsession to the person who betrayed you. Hellbent on getting even, you spend so long in the role of victim that your energies are depleted and you miss vital opportunities for personal growth.

In fact, as long as you hold on to vengeful feelings of any kind, your betrayer will have power over you. By carrying a grudge, you allow the past to control you, and you avoid the tough emotional work of healing, which you really must do in order to move on. Revenge becomes hazardous to your emotional health. By refusing to forget the past, you obliterate any potential for a promising future.

How Sweet It Is

There is, however, one way in which revenge can be constructive: when it motivates you to prove your worth and prompts you to proclaim, like the character in the movie *Network,* "I'm mad as hell, and I'm not going to take it anymore!" When, in the aftermath of a betrayal of trust, you begin to feel, "I count; I do matter"—and set out to prove, to yourself and others, that you are indeed worthy of love and trust—then, and only then, can revenge be a positive force.

The saying "Living well is the best revenge" expresses the simple fact that in order to avenge an act of broken trust, you don't need to destroy your betrayer. Rather, you need to enhance yourself and your life. Instead of looking for ways to strike back, strike out on your own and strengthen yourself. Sharpen your confrontational skills. In the next chapter, I'll explain how you can stand up to someone who has betrayed your trust.

But remember the most important rule of revenge: never

compromise your integrity by taking an action that can ultimately ruin your life. Lynn, the urban planner we met a few pages back, finally found a new position at another engineering firm and was able to leave her ruthless boss behind. Several years later, she was asked by a headhunter to give an evaluation of her old boss, who was applying for a top-level position. Lynn told the truth, and the other woman didn't get the job.

"She never knew what I did . . . in fact, I never saw her again," Lynn recalled with a smile. "But I'll be honest: it sure felt great. Truth *is* the best revenge."

C H A P T E R 8

To Confront or Not to Confront?

What to Say, What to Do in a Trust Crisis

If revenge is anger raging out of control, then confrontation is one way to channel that anger constructively. In fact, when trust is broken, confrontation is a healthy and often necessary step. It can restore your battered self-esteem and arm you against future hurts. It may also be the only opportunity you have to take an up-close look at what occurred, to hold the person who broke your trust accountable for his actions, and, most important, to get a picture of what role you may have played in the breakdown of trust.

For the fact is this: if you've experienced a breach of trust, you share some responsibility for the betrayal. You didn't do anything wrong; it wasn't "your fault"; and you shouldn't blame yourself. But you did miss some cues along the way. On some level, you were a participant, albeit unintentionally, in your own trust crisis. You must find out why it happened so that you can forge balanced, truly trusting relationships in the future.

Confrontation can also be a caring step. As I noted in Chapter 3, there may be times when people are genuinely unaware that they've betrayed you. By confronting them, you help raise their level of consciousness and restore an important relationship that might otherwise disintegrate under the weight of misunderstanding.

But confrontation is tough. In the wake of betrayal, most people don't know what to do. Shell-shocked, paralyzed by disbelief, and flooded with anger, they find it difficult to register what has happened, let alone figure out what went wrong or what to do next. They wonder, "Should I speak up and let the person who let me down know exactly what he did and how I feel? Or should I say nothing and try to forget the whole thing? Besides, what can I possibly say that won't make me appear foolish or make the situation even more unbearable?"

When someone breaks a trust, you have several choices. You can confront the person directly about the betrayal. You can avoid the confrontation but change the way you relate to that person. Or you can walk away from the relationship and end all contact with that person. But you cannot ignore a breach of trust. The price, in terms of your self-confidence and self-esteem, is just too high. While there is no guarantee that confrontation will bring about a resolution to your trust crisis, pushing it aside, ignoring it, or trying to forget what happened, leaves unfinished business that will almost always haunt you.

LEARNING TO SPEAK UP

Unfortunately, no matter how wounding the betrayal, most people don't say or do what they want to, for a variety of reasons. Many people are confused about what it means to confront. Confronting doesn't mean fighting with someone; it simply means addressing what went on, speaking up.

Perhaps you were raised in a punitive, critical household, where feelings were rarely considered and emotions were stifled. If so, you may believe you're not entitled to be angry in the first place. For you, any disagreement has the potential to tap into old insecurities and fears. You'd rather ignore a breach of trust than call attention to it.

Perhaps you shy away from confrontation because you're too angry and flustered. Anger is a shield that protects you from the pain and loss that accompany a betrayal of trust. The trouble is that when the anger is not dissipated, it can trigger an array of physical and psychological symptoms, from neck and back pain to gastrointestinal upsets, to depression.

And finally, you may keep quiet because you're afraid of the other person's reaction. With egos already on the line, and your self-esteem dealt a serious blow, why risk further damage? You may fear that the confrontation will lead to combat and that you'll be further battered. Or you may worry that you'll be let down once again if the person denies what he did, lies about what really happened, or, worse, admits he betrayed your trust because he never cared about you in the first place.

In fact, people often tell me they avoid confronting hurtful behavior because they fear the other person's angry response, or they are so distressed by the other person's anger that they back down and retreat. They may also be afraid of the consequences: the confronted person may retaliate, turn others against you, or reject you again. You can gain courage by practicing in front of a mirror, talking it out in front of another person, or even using a tape recorder.

WHY CONFRONTATION IS CRITICAL: FOUR TALES FROM THE TRENCHES

Confrontation serves several purposes, and each is fueled by the need to understand why the person you trusted could do this to you. Confrontation provides a means for managing the negative feelings churning inside you. By calling the other person on their behavior, you will hear his reasons for his unscrupulous actions. Even if those answers are not what you want to hear, even if he remains silent, you'll learn something important from the experience that you can use in future relationships. You can then make an informed decision about whether to mend or end the relationship.

For a confrontation to be successful, however, you must be clear about your purpose. Before you begin, reflect on three points: whether you are going to be open-minded and make your decision based on the way the other person responds; whether you are going to try to repair the damage and redefine the relationship; or whether you want to sever the relationship entirely. Let's check back with some of the people we met in earlier chapters to see how they handled their trust crisis confrontations.

Eliot's Story

Eliot, the business man we met in Chapter 5 who was dumb-struck to learn that his childhood friend, Barry, a college professor, had failed to write the promised letter of recommendation for his son, was open to reconciliation.

"Barry and I have known each other for thirty years," he told me. "We've shared every important event in our lives; he's been like a brother to me, and even my parents considered him a part of our family. I wanted to salvage that friendship." But when Eliot called Barry and asked why he not only didn't follow through but had also lied about it, Barry was silent.

"If he'd apologized, or even stammered some feeble excuse, I probably could have remained friends," Eliot said philosophically. "But he didn't say one word, and that made my blood boil. It would have been an easy thing for him to do. I feel he betrayed us all." Barry's failure to respond was further proof to Eliot of his blatant disregard for him and his family. Eliot hasn't spoken to Barry since, and doesn't plan to.

Linda's Story

Linda, whom we met in Chapter 1, saw confrontation as an opportunity to reframe and redefine her relationship with Tom, her long-time colleague and friend. Initially, Linda confronted Tom and angrily blamed him for going behind her back. Not surprisingly, Tom defended his actions, and Linda backed off.

During the next few weeks, Linda spurned Tom's overtures.

She realized that she had overlooked many of his self-serving actions in the past—the way he relied on her to tie up the loose ends of projects they were supposed to complete jointly and the way he made her lose valuable working time when he was consistently late. But as she thought about what happened, she realized she did value his friendship at work. What's more, his continued efforts to apologize showed good faith on his part. Then, too, she could see that pieces of the relationship were valuable to her. "Since we were in the same field, it made sense to stay on good terms with him," Linda explained. "I don't mean this in a cynical way, but why burn bridges if I could learn instead to handle the situation differently?"

These realizations gave Linda the strength to confront Tom again. She asked him to meet for a drink after work, and this time, she took a different tack. Instead of accusing Tom, she approached him with an open mind. "Why didn't you tell me first?" she asked. This time, Tom responded differently, too. "You're right," he said softly. "I wish I had told you. I was conflicted, and I felt guilty. I thought I had made the right decision, but now I see I didn't."

Linda's second confrontation was successful, because, by first asking questions instead of hurling accusations, she gave Tom room to apologize and take responsibility for what he had done. Second, she was able to use her anger constructively to set limits for herself. She did this by becoming less available and no longer overextending herself. She stopped going out of her way to help Tom. If he was more than five minutes late for a scheduled meeting, she left. By editing the personal friendship out of her work relationship, she was able to preserve her connection with Tom on a level that was comfortable for her. Most important, she no longer felt like a victim.

Clear in her own mind about how she wanted the relationship to continue, she rebuilt it on her own terms.

Loni's Story

Then there are those people who confront a betrayer with the clear intention of severing the relationship. Another client of mine, Loni, had been friends with Carol for fifteen years, but as far as Loni was concerned, it was an uneasy, one-sided friendship. Each time Loni called Carol on her actions, she'd reply, "Well, you know that's how I am." For years, Loni seethed silently—until the day she had to call on Carol to pick up a package from the apartment of a mutual friend. Not surprisingly, Carol forgot—and Loni reached her limit. After a cold war of four weeks, during which time she refused to return Carol's calls, Loni wrote her a short, succinct letter.

"I told her I was tired of how she was never there for me, never willing to extend herself on my behalf. Though she hadn't acted any differently this time than she had a thousand times before, I decided I just didn't want to remain friends," Loni reported to me. "Carol got upset and started to cry," Loni continued. "She apologized and promised it wouldn't happen again. But I'd been giving her the benefit of the doubt for many years, and I no longer believed she had the ability to change." Even though Loni accepted Carol's apology, she used her anger to examine her expectations for friendship, and she realized that Carol no longer measured up. "The light bulb suddenly went on. I simply didn't want her in my life anymore."

Myra's Story

On the other hand, some people tiptoe around a confrontation for a long time, trying to avoid it, until the betrayals became so unbearable, they feel compelled to say something. Take Myra—who, as we saw in Chapter 5, had wrapped her life and that of her family around her friendship with the narcissistic Sophia. Myra wanted to find out why Sophia treated her so badly, in the hope that she could straighten things out and repair the damage. Instead, she discovered that the relationship meant far less to Sophia than it did to her.

"I felt like such a fool," Myra said, recalling the time she confronted Sophia about her selfishness. "I was feeling so vulnerable, and she stepped all over me, telling me I was too clingy. To tell you the truth, I don't think I would have believed she said it if I hadn't heard it from her directly. I had to see her face, have her tell me outright that the relationship really meant nothing to her. That was the only way I was going to get it through my thick head."

If, like Myra, you've experienced a breach of trust so profound, you may find the rebuilding process slow and the fear of confrontation great. However, confrontation may be the only way you can free yourself from an untrustworthy relationship and see that the expectations you have for friendship—that is, the trust factors we discussed in Chapter 2—clash dramatically with someone else's. Like Myra, you may need to hear your betrayer himself present the justification for deceitful behavior, his sense of entitlement, or the fact that, left to his own devices, he'd do it again. Only then will you believe that you are better off without him.

Remember, the purpose of confrontation is to convey your feelings so clearly that the other person appreciates the effect his actions have had on you. So where do you begin? In the following section, I've outlined a four-step Confrontation Strategy for dealing with any breach of trust, whether it's by a Rival, an Admirer, or a User. The strategy gives you the words, and the mindset, to begin a discussion with your betrayer, to redesign the relationship so that it meets your needs, or to end the relationship and feel good about that, too.

TALK TACTICS: MAKING IT HAPPEN

Before you begin, you must size up the situation. This is the time when you determine whether or not you want to confront your betrayer directly. You decide which course of action is best for you by carefully assessing the nature of the betrayal. First, gauge whether you are dealing with a Rival, an Admirer, or a User. Then determine what kind of betrayal it was: a lie, a rumor, an assault on your character, or an attempt to sabotage your success. Consider, too, whether it was a direct or indirect breach of trust. You may have become upset over hearsay, which you can't really prove. When sizing up the situation, you must also reflect on the nature of your relations with the person who betrayed you. Consider the following questions to help you size up the situation:

- Is your betrayer very important to you? Is she or he a spouse or lover? A close relative? An old friend or colleague?
- Is it essential that this person continue to be involved in your life? Do you work for, or with, this person, making your relations critical to your financial survival?
- Do you share a long history that's worth maintaining? Do you value him and want him in your life, even in a limited way?
- When you're with this person, do you feel good about yourself? Does he treat you with respect, the way you want to be treated?
- Are there other people in your life who will be hurt by the change in your relationship (for example, family or friends)?

If you answer *yes* to most of these questions, then confrontation is probably the wisest step for you to take to preserve the relationship. If you answer *no* to most of the questions, confrontation may not be warranted. You may instead opt for ending the relationship. Eliot, for instance, was highly motivated to initiate a confrontation, because Barry had an old relationship with both him and his family.

Now you are ready to use the three-step Confrontation Strategy.

Step 1: Determine the Motive

By determining the motive, you can understand why your betrayer acted the way she did. In other words, how could she do this to you? In the future, you will be more aware that another person may try to manipulate you when you are most vulnerable. You can then guard against betraying behavior and sidestep it before it occurs.

The key to Step 1 is to remain genuinely curious about what the person tells you. Your objective is to learn *her* truth, not to try to convince her of your truth. When you confront your betrayer, describe objectively what happened. You could begin by saying, "You told me you weren't going to repeat anything I said, and then you told the boss."

In this first step, you want to find out where she was coming from. Does she rationalize and justify her self-serving behavior? Does she genuinely believe she was helping you? The pitfall in this step is that many people tend automatically to attach malicious motives to the other person's actions before giving her a chance to tell her side.

For example, instead of saying, "You only think about yourself," or "You didn't want to do the work so you dumped it on me," you should present your understanding of your current relationship as well as what you perceive to have been the breach of trust. Remember, her response may not make any sense to you, but it does to her, and that's what you have to deal with.

Step 2: Express Your Feelings Clearly

Most people assume that confrontation is inherently negative and should be avoided at all costs. But confrontation is neither combat nor a contest. Step 2 in a successful confrontation involves talking about yourself and the way you feel about the betrayal. Many people tend to talk only about what the other person did, but that usually starts an argument or elicits a defensive reaction.

For example: "When you [state what happened: lied to me, didn't write the recommendation] I felt [state how you felt or still feel about what happened: disappointed, hurt, and shocked] that you didn't follow through."

Then, too, most people don't know how to describe their feelings. They think that simply beginning a conversation with an "I" statement is enough. However, "I feel you're an idiot" is not what I mean by an honest expression of your feelings. That's criticism, and criticism is inflammatory. Better: "When you didn't support me at that meeting, I felt you were against me."

In Step 2, you must listen to your betrayer and, hard as it seems, try to empathize with her. Reflect on what you hear and be open to her point of view. You may say, "Let me think about it, I didn't realize that."

Step 3: Set Limits

The most difficult task in confronting a betrayer—and the step where most confrontations get derailed—is staying focused on your objective: the actions you want taken and the behaviors you will no longer tolerate. When you find yourself faced with an array of hostile reactions, it's hard to respond to them. Use the following as a guide:

IF YOU ENCOUNTER FLAT-OUT DENIAL:

"I didn't do it." "Where did you get that idea?" "That's not what happened at all."

Your knee-jerk reaction is to persist in the face of denial. But the more you insist you're right, the more your betrayer will dig in his heels. If possible, check out the situation with other people to make sure you are not overreacting or misinterpreting events. If what you discover is consistent with the person's past behavior, hold on to your feelings and insist that those feelings be addressed.

THEN YOU CAN SAY:

"I'm not going to debate the facts with you. The bottom line is, I believe you betrayed my confidence by revealing personal information about me. If you care at all about me, won't you take the opportunity now to be honest with me?"

IF YOU ENCOUNTER A PUT-DOWN:

"You're ridiculous." "You're just too sensitive."

Don't allow yourself to be talked out of your feelings because of your own insecurities or doubts. Instead, set limits.

THEN YOU CAN SAY:

"I won't continue to talk to you if you insist on insulting me and refuse to take my feelings seriously."

IF YOU ENCOUNTER BLAME AND ANGER:

"Where the hell do you get off thinking I'd ever do something like that?" "How could you say that to me?"

Take a deep breath and try to stay calm. Avoid being oppositional even while you maintain your feelings and reiterate your point.

THEN YOU CAN SAY:

"I'm not trying to blame you, but I felt let down the time you didn't defend me when the others made those cutting remarks." "You may not see it this way, but I felt disappointed when you didn't support my proposal after we talked about it." If she continues to stay angry, you must say, "Maybe when you cool off, we can continue talking about what's upsetting me." Walk away until she does cool off.

IF YOU ENCOUNTER NO REMORSE OR A DEFIANT CHALLENGE:

"So what if I said that, what right do you have to be upset?"

This reaction is telling you to put the brakes on your relationship. This person doesn't care enough about you, your feelings, or the relationship.

THEN YOU CAN SAY:

"If you really think that what you did was okay, or that there wasn't anything hurtful in your actions, then you're telling me you don't care. That's important for me to know. That tells me where I stand . . . and what our relationship really is."

IF YOU ENCOUNTER A SPIN DOCTOR:

This rationalizer is clearly not relating to your feelings at all. He prefers to put his own take on everything or even flip the blame back to you by saying, "Well, what about what you did?" Again, make sure you don't get bulldozed.

Then You Can Say:

"That may be true, and I'm willing to address it, but first we need to address this, since I started the discussion." "I hear what you're saying, and it may make sense to you. But the bottom line is, I still feel bad about what you did—and I don't get the impression that you care."

Though these comments may feel awkward or sound silly at first, remember that it takes time to change your behavior, too. After a while, you will feel more comfortable, and your thoughts will automatically shift into this new gear. Meanwhile, practice your responses—in front of a mirror or with a trusted friend, or even by reciting into a tape recorder—until the words, and the feelings behind the words, seem natural to you. The point is not to let the other person derail you by countering, negating, or justifying his behavior. Hold onto what you know and feel and use it.

When Confrontations Boomerang

It's important to understand that not every betrayal of trust can or should be confronted. We all have potential battles looming on our horizons, but with limited time and energy, who has the wherewithal to fight every one of them? As I said, challenging a breach of trust does involve risks, and those need to be assessed first. Will a confrontation make the situation worse . . . or will things become worse if you remain silent? Pick your battles carefully so that you avoid a confrontation's backfiring.

Before you launch a confrontation, think about what you expect to happen afterward and what's at stake. Determine whether the issue is more important than the potential fallout. In fact, de-

ciding *not* to confront may actually be the emotionally healthy—
and smart—thing to do. Consider the following situations:

Someone Stabs You in the Back
at Work

Every workplace has tales of colleagues stealing another's ideas
or making snide remarks about another's competence. While
it's critical to protect your turf and your reputation on the job,
confrontation may not be the wisest step every time.

Remember Jerry, the producer we met in Chapter 4? He
had just discovered that Chris, a trusted colleague at the radio
station where he worked, had failed to give him a favorable
recommendation. Angry, Jerry first intended to tell Chris exactly how he felt. After assessing the situation, however, he decided not to confront him. "I realized I really didn't have a
solid case to prove that he had screwed me," Jerry said. "What
I'd learned, I'd heard through a third party. I had no proof."
The experience put him on guard and taught him to be more
careful in the future about where he placed his trust.

The bottom line: If you directly overhear another person
badmouthing you or your work, by all means confront the
person. Calmly and firmly say, "What do you mean by that re-
mark? Why didn't you check it out with me first?" Even if a
backstabber denies her action, she will probably stop, since
being exposed is the worst thing that could happen to such a
reputation sniper.

But if you can't prove the accusations, your path is not as
clear. First, consider whom you're dealing with. If your bad-
mouther is known as the office dragon, someone who never

has a kind word to say about anyone and is loud and aggressive with everyone, then try not to take her comments personally. She may be well connected to the powers that be, and you may be better off choosing another tactic. Save your resources and cultivate the friendship of people in the office you know you can trust. At the same time, protect yourself by editing your conversations more carefully so that you know exactly what you're saying and to whom you're saying it.

When the Timing Isn't Right

Another instance when you may be smarter choosing not to challenge a betrayal—at least not just then—is when the person who let you down is going through a difficult period or transition in her own life. Remember Cynthia and Sybil, the best friends we met in Chapter 4? Cynthia felt that her friend was never there for her, now that she had a new baby. However, after months of feeling hurt and angry, Cynthia decided not to confront Sybil.

The bottom line: Anytime someone is going through a major life change—even a joyful one, such as having a baby, starting a new job, moving to a new city—it may be difficult for her to reach out to others. As a friend, you should appreciate the changes she is going through and, though it hurts, wait until after she has negotiated the transition before you assess the damage and evaluate the status of your relationship. If Cynthia had confronted Sybil right then about her lack of availability, Sybil might have experienced the pressure as yet another demand and reacted with anger.

"I had to deal with my own feelings. Besides, what could I really say?" Cynthia said in retrospect. "Talking negatively about her was only making things worse. I realized that to save our friendship, I had to accept the change that her new relationship brought. Sybil's feelings for me hadn't changed, but the demands on her had." By carving out a new place for herself, Cynthia preserved the friendship—and her own self-esteem.

In such circumstances, you don't have to squash your feelings entirely. If Cynthia's resentment was interfering with the time she did spend with Sybil, then she needed to confront her in a caring way, by saying, "I know this is a busy time for you, and I don't want to add to the demands, but I need to know that our friendship is still important to you." Then her friend can confirm that it is, and give her the reassurance she needs.

When It Affects Other People

At other times, to keep things peaceful, you may choose not to confront someone—especially if the results of your confrontation will spill over into other relationships and involve people like children, other family members, or colleagues. That's why Abby finally chose not to confront her cousin Robin, with whom she'd had a long and hurtful rivalry. Though barely able to contain her fury, Abby nevertheless decided that the impact of such a confrontation on her extended family—including her controlling mother and aunt—was more than she was prepared to deal with.

"Someone else might say I chickened out," said Abby, "but I don't see it that way. I did what I had to do to preserve my emotional strength. I chose instead to freeze Robin out of my

CONFRONTATION CUES

DO ask questions to check out a betrayer's intention.
DON'T criticize or make assumptions about what his motivation may have been.
DO use tact and good listening skills to hear him out.
DON'T expect or assume that the other person will know how you feel or what you mean. You must take responsibility for verbalizing your feelings.
DO tell him the effect that his recent behavior has had on you.
DON'T generalize or pile on a laundry list of past grievances.
DO use verbal brakes to end a confrontation when the conversation gets too heated.

life. Now, I don't talk to her except in the most superficial way, and, amazingly, the things she does and says honestly don't bother me."

Remember: learning to confront effectively is a skill, and like any other, it takes time to master. To overcome your fear, you have to chisel away at it little by little, until you are clear about your goals and satisfied with the outcome.

CHAPTER 9

Are You Really Sorry?

The Healing Power of an Apology

Overcoming the pain of betrayal takes time, but how long is up to you. As you learned in the previous chapter, confrontation is the first step in the healing process. By confronting, you express your anger in such a way that the person who broke your trust can understand how you feel. Confrontation allows you to examine your relationship and figure out what went wrong and why; you hope, too, that it will force the person who betrayed you to take responsibility for his behavior.

The next step—and it's a big one—is learning to forgive your betrayer and move on.

The decision to forgive is not easily made or quickly

achieved. Learning to forgive is a gradual process, not an isolated event; it can benefit both the betrayed and the betrayer. You can't simply forget the heartbreak of a betrayal. But when you forgive the person who betrayed you, you free up the emotional and physical energy you need to feel whole once again. At the same time, you motivate your betrayer to change his behavior so that, if you choose to, you can salvage the relationship on your own terms.

For many people, the key to forgiveness is merely hearing the apology of the person who wronged them. A heartfelt apology—strictly defined as a statement expressing regret for a fault or offense—is one of the most significant actions that can take place between two people. When you're burning with anger over a betrayal, it can be the fire extinguisher that smothers the flame. An apology genuinely offered and graciously accepted has the power to validate hurt feelings and restore even the most seriously damaged relationships.

But what if that apology never comes? Despite its healing power, a true apology is a rare commodity these days. Most of us don't know how or when to offer—or to receive—an apology. In this fast-paced, competitive world, many people see no alternative but to look out for themselves at the expense of others.

Then, too, as experts have pointed out, women tend to apologize too much and too often, while men are loath to admit their guilt. No doubt such behavior can be traced right back to the playground, where girls learn early to nurture friendships and be the caretakers of relationships. As they grow up, women tend to be more empathic and remain more at ease talking about their feelings. Little boys, on the other hand, are encouraged to buck up and get on with it. Men often have trouble offering an apology because it makes them feel vulnerable, an emotion they usually try to avoid.

It's hard to tell when an apology is sincere. It is equally difficult to slash through your pain and mistrust and to truly believe that the person who wronged you will, indeed, change. An apology may be genuinely offered, but you may still be too angry to hear it, let alone accept it. Can you ever risk trusting again?

LOVE MEANS HAVING TO SAY YOU'RE SORRY

Contrary to that oft-quoted line from the tear-jerker book and film *Love Story,* love does *not* mean never having to say you're sorry. However, for a host of reasons, many people never apologize, no matter how major their infraction.

Some unwitting betrayers fail to apologize because they actually believe they were helping you. Owning up to the fact that, despite their good intentions, they did do something wrong becomes, in their mind, tantamount to saying, "There's something wrong with me." Pride compels these people to take a stubborn stance and deny that they may have acted in a hypocritical, unscrupulous manner.

Caroline, an assistant buyer for an upscale department store, is one of these people. Planning a New Year's Eve party, she failed to invite her college roommate, Anita, who had quit her job to stay home with her baby daughter. "I don't think she'd fit in with this crowd," Caroline told herself. When Anita heard about the party from a friend, she confronted Caroline and told her how hurt she was.

"I've invited her to every party or dinner I ever had," Anita explained. "I can't tell you how hurt I was that she thought I wasn't hip enough to associate with her crowd." Caroline hemmed and hawed but still refused to say the two simple words that would have saved their ten-year friendship. When Anita continued to press for an apology, Caroline blurted out, "I can't. I just can't say it." That's when Anita said, "I don't understand. Doesn't our friendship mean anything to you?" At which point Caroline replied, "Of course it does. You're the most important friend I have . . . but saying I'm sorry makes me feel so ashamed. It reminds me of how humiliated and powerless I used to feel when my father forced me to apologize for every squabble I had with my sister." Because Caroline was so open, Anita was able to understand and stay friends.

Then there are those people who genuinely believe they've done nothing to warrant your anger. "You don't have any right to be mad at me," they may reply indignantly. These people often operate under the misguided notion that to apologize means to admit guilt. While this may be true at times, it is certainly not always the case. If someone is too proud to admit a mistake—if he's focused on being right rather than on making things right again in the relationship—apologizing will make him feel weak. In truth, sometimes an apology is a way to show concern for another's distress, "I'm really sorry that you're so hurt that I didn't call you, but that's the way it is for me right now."

Others, like Meredith (the investment banking executive we met in Chapter 3, who was convinced her friend Beverly was after her job), may feel their options were so limited that they had no choice but to act as they did. Boxed into a corner, they react with bewilderment when you get upset about their behavior. They'll try to get you to understand their point of view at the same time as they're apologizing to you, but often the apology gets drowned out. Their hallmark reply is: "I'm sorry, but . . ."

Some betrayers only see things their way. They may say, "I'm sorry you're mad at me," but really mean, "I'm sorry that *you* don't like *me.*" These people specialize in false apologies; their objective is to regain your support, not to acknowledge their wrongdoing.

At times, people may also feel justified in withholding an apology, as retaliation for something they feel you began in the first place. We see this many times when office politics and rivals in romance badmouth each other in a steamrolling tit-for-tat. "Apologize? What for?" they argue. "You brought this on yourself. You got what you deserved." Other people don't apologize because they sense it will be futile: "What's the point," they think; "she's only going to get angrier. Why bother?"

And, finally, there are those betrayers who, paralyzed by guilt, avoid an apology because making one would require that they take a hard look at their values, beliefs, and behavior. That may be too shameful to bear. It would mean admitting that their greed or their needs led them to violate you. To escape the personal humiliation, they avoid you in every way.

THE APOLOGY

For an apology to be meaningful, a betrayer cannot gloss over the incident and merely mumble, "I'm sorry." Rather, he must account for his actions, acknowledge your specific griev-ances, and empathize with how you are feeling. Empathy is key; it is what allows a betrayer to prove that he understands the pain you have suffered and is remorseful. Empathy can mark the difference between a relationship that flourishes and one that withers, whether it's a romance or a friendship.

A satisfactory apology must be said in words. The fact that Howard Brant—who had an affair with the wife of his brother Jeff and eventually married her—never actually said, "I'm sorry," was at the center of a cold war that bitterly divided the extended family for nearly a decade. Though Howard tried to make amends in other ways, until Jeff actually heard him say the words "I'm sorry," he couldn't even begin to heal the breach.

The power of those words also affected Eliot, whom we met in Chapter 5. Eliot admitted that if his friend Barry, who failed to write the recommendation letter for his son, had said he was sorry, "I could have forgiven him. Things wouldn't have been the same between us, but at least we would have remained friends. But he couldn't even spit out those two little words." And so a lifelong friendship disintegrated.

For an apology to be satisfactory, the betrayer must acknowledge his wrongdoing and take responsibility for his behavior. This means not making excuses or trying to justify his actions. An apology must also speak to the future; it must be seen as a promise that a similar incident won't happen again, and must outline the steps a betrayer will take to make sure that it doesn't. As Tom said to Linda in Chapter 1, "I'm sorry I didn't talk to you before taking the job. I know you felt hurt, and in the future I'll always check it out with you before I do anything."

Finally, an apology must be followed by some repair work; that is, a demonstration of better behavior. The betrayer must extend himself in some way, perhaps by offering financial reimbursement or a token gift. If the situation warrants, he may even make a public apology, demonstrating openly that he is indeed sorry.

Needless to say, the timing of an apology is critical. If you receive an apology before you've had a chance to vent your rage or despair, it may seem to you insincere, like lip service. If an apology is delayed too long, you will probably feel neglected.

WHEN THE APOLOGY IS NOT ENOUGH

Sometimes an apology doesn't work at all. Instead of soothing your anger, it turns up the flame by validating your sense of having been wronged.

Remember Ian, whose rivalry with his best friend, Kenny, became paramount and destroyed their friendship? Ian felt betrayed and displaced once Kenny assumed a prominent position in the lives of his sister and her young children. On a national television show, in which I was the expert psychotherapist, Ian and Kenny came together to hash out what was going on. When Kenny apologized and asked, "Can't we be friends again?" Ian jumped from his seat, grabbed Kenny by the shirt collar, and began to choke him. He didn't calm down until the security guards intervened. What was going on? Kenny's words had validated Ian's right to be angry. Ian felt so wounded by the perceived loss of his relationship with his sister that the apology seemed to confirm Kenny's having done something terrible to him.

In fact, some people harbor so many grievances that when the long-awaited apology finally comes, it opens the flood-

THE ART OF FORGIVENESS

1. Stay focused on the present situation. Don't bring up old war wounds.

2. Acknowledge and support small efforts. Allow time for change; it doesn't happen overnight.

3. Don't belittle the changes that have occurred, even though they may not yet be as great as you would like them to be.

4. Resist the temptation to blame yourself for what happened, or you will continue to experience fallout from the betrayal that will block your path to forgiveness.

5. If you sincerely want to forgive, let go of the mantra "It's too little, too late." Soon, it really will be too late.

gates of resentment. Refusing to accept an apology makes people feel self-righteous, powerful, and in control. They may even revel in their role as a victim and use an apology as an opportunity to resurrect old incidents in which they felt hurt or betrayed.

Rick launched just such a character assassination of his brother Lawrence, who he believed had stolen his girlfriend. Furious, Rick refused to see or talk to either Lawrence or the woman. One day, the brothers bumped into each other at their mother's house, and when Lawrence again said he was sorry and tried to repair the relationship, Rick spewed forth a string of insults: "Sorry? Yeah, I bet you're sorry. You're about as sorry as you were when you chased after that girl in high school who really liked me until you put the moves on her. And what about that guy you double-crossed at work two years ago, shoving him aside as you clawed your way up the career ladder? My friends warned me about you. You're a liar. No one trusts you, Lawrence; no one." Lawrence's pleas and attempts to make amends fell on deaf ears. Rick didn't want to forgive. He wanted to punish.

For people like Ian and Rick, it is essential to hold up a shield of anger, and to refuse to accept an apology as a way of protecting themselves from further pain. You may believe that the apology offered is too little, too late. Heartfelt though it may sound, you can be too convinced that the person ruined your life; you cannot forgive and trust him again. Under these circumstances, your accepting an apology may appear to condone what your betrayer did.

LEARNING TO FORGIVE

Forgiveness is the conscious decision you make to move past betrayal, to heal your wounds, and, if you choose, to preserve the relationship. By forgiving, you take control of your life and make a statement, to yourself and others, that you will no longer remain in the grip of past betrayals. It is a choice you make to restore faith and, if possible, rebuild trust.

Learning to forgive and forget is an individual experience. Everyone's healing process is different, and the emotional devastation you feel after your trust has been broken obviously depends on the type of betrayal and how much you valued the relationship in the first place. Some people are able to move beyond their anger quickly; for others, it can take years. Never push or rush the forgiveness process or berate yourself for the length of time you need to heal.

And don't accept an apology for the wrong reasons. Because of the fear of losing a relationship, the desire to feel noble, or simply to give someone the benefit of the doubt, a person may be motivated to accept an apology too quickly, throwing a monkey wrench into the healing process. Valerie is a case in point. In her effort to give her boyfriend a chance to prove his trustworthiness, she repeatedly accepted flippant and insincere apologies. For her, forgiveness came too easily, without any proven changes in his behavior. She fell victim to broken trust, time and again.

When your trust in someone is broken, you will inevitably experience shock, denial, anger, and sadness, feelings that are, in many ways, akin to the mourning process following a death. After all, a betrayal of trust is like a death; it is the loss not only of that person in your life, but also of all that person represented. If she was an integral part of your world, it may be necessary to find a way to forgive her. That's what Jenny did in Chapter 4. Though she was devastated to learn that her roommate had slept with her boyfriend, she felt compelled to find the strength to forgive. To Jenny, these two people were her "whole world." The thought of living a life without them was more than she could bear.

In order to accept an apology, you must take time to understand exactly how this person hurt you. Was your pride wounded? Your self-esteem shaken? Did you feel rejected, unloved, humiliated? As I discussed earlier, consider also the motivation of the person who betrayed you. Once you understand why he did what he did, and can view your betrayer more realistically, you will have a clearer picture of the kind of repair work you must do in order to resume the relationship.

To forgive and go forward, you must also be able to balance your betrayer's good and bad qualities. Be open to what he has to say. See whether you can accept him as he is, limitations, weaknesses, and all. Learn to tolerate your uncertainty while you watch for real signs of behavioral change.

Kira struggled with this dilemma. Though her husband of four years, Joel, had ended a brief affair with someone he'd met at work, Kira remained angry, suspicious, and mistrustful. The couple were in marital counseling with me, during which we'd resolved many underlying issues that had contributed to Joel's infidelity. Joel had said, over and over, how sorry he was, and promised he'd never again be unfaithful. And in every possible way, he tried to demonstrate his remorse by being loving and attentive to his wife. Still, Kira could not erase the memory of the affair.

"If I go out to pick up the Sunday paper, she thinks I'm sneaking a phone call," Joel reports. "She's totally paranoid. So I told her, 'I won't get the paper. If it's going to upset you, it's not that important.'" During one counseling session by himself, Joel asked me what else he could do to regain Kira's trust. I told him: "You're doing the right thing by reassuring her with your actions. But remember, it may take Kira a long time to let go of her anger. Until then, you must muster all your patience not to react when she gets upset and to continue to demonstrate your trustworthiness."

The point is that even a betrayal of enormous magnitude—infidelity, chronic substance abuse, gambling, as well as physical or verbal abuse—can in time be forgiven as long as the betrayal is followed by a sincere expression of remorse and a consistent and lasting behavioral change.

Eventually, Kira did forgive Joel. In counseling, she also worked hard to examine the role she had played in some of the marital problems. But it was a slow and painful recovery that would not have succeeded had it not been for Joel's unwavering commitment to restoring his wife's trust.

Sometimes forgiveness can take longer. Max kept his distance from his childhood buddy Bruce for more than five years after Bruce had borrowed money from him. He'd told Max it was for his new business, but he used it to make a downpayment on a vacation condo. Max was livid, but Bruce was strangely unrepentant. When Max asked Bruce to repay him, Bruce replied, "Why? You don't need the money. Your law practice is huge, and after that merger you pulled off last month, you're in great shape." Then he added, "You don't really care about my happiness, do you?" The classic narcissist, Bruce felt entitled—and Max was furious.

But Max's ex-wife was a close friend of Bruce's, and when she was diagnosed with an inoperable brain tumor, she asked Bruce to look after her children when she died. Over the next few years, Bruce became a surrogate uncle to Max's twelve-year-old twin sons, taking them to concerts, plays, and sports events. Whenever they needed help—in school, with friends, or applying for summer internships—Bruce was there.

Five years later, Max relented and accepted Bruce's overture to meet for a drink. "I still have misgivings and I don't trust him," he told me recently, "but how can you not forgive a person who's been so terrific to your kids?" Max wasn't willing to renew the friendship, but because of his former friend's consistent attempts to prove himself trustworthy, he was, on some level, able to forgive.

Until forgiveness is possible, quell your feelings of insecurity and self-doubt by putting a time limit on self-blame. Take responsibility for the role you may have played in the betrayal, but forgive yourself, too. Recognize when you're slipping into that litany of self-recrimination: "If only I had" . . . "If only I hadn't" . . . "I wish I had." Instead, force yourself to say, midsentence, "Maybe I should have done such-and-such, but everyone makes mistakes. I made mine, and now it's time to leave them behind."

Remember, too, that you can decide to forgive a betrayal of trust and still choose to end your relationship, especially if you've been tolerant for a long time. Like Loni, who broke off her friendship with Carol after the latter consistently failed to come through for her, you can forgive—and then let go.

However, before you can trust again, you must be able to trust yourself—to rely on your intuition, your awareness, and your judgment. In the next chapter, I'll explain the lessons you need to learn, and the new tools you can use, to help you achieve this goal.

CHAPTER 10

Now You Know: Trusting Yourself;

Lessons to Live By

No matter who has betrayed you, or in what way, you will be too emotionally scarred—and scared—to trust again. Mistrustful and suspicious, you may back away, not only from the person who has wronged you, but also from other relationships. Myriad thoughts may race through your head: "Whom can I trust? Why was I so stupid?" Or you may slip into a denial mode, refusing to believe that your betrayer acted maliciously, and trying to rationalize hurtful actions by convincing yourself that "this couldn't possibly happen again."

But the truth is, it *will* happen again—unless you take several steps right now to protect yourself. Repeatedly, people ask

me, "How can I ever learn to trust somebody again?" My answer is twofold: by learning to trust yourself and by knowing
what to look for in others. To do this:

- You need to understand why you fell victim to betrayal.
- You need to make sure that your expectations in every
  relationship are appropriate and practical.
- You need to identify your emotional needs and rebuild
  your self-esteem.
- You need to define what I call your Trust Bottom Line.
  Later in this chapter, I will show you how to set
  effective limits so that you can take care of yourself.
- You need to trust your gut feelings and your own
  judgment.

Once you understand these fundamental tasks, you *will* be
able to trust again—not blindly, not hesitantly, but knowingly.
Let the following lessons be your guide.

LESSONS TO LIVE BY

1. Draw Your Trust Profile

As I discussed earlier, the family in which you grew up affected
how trusting you are today. By taking a look at the ways in
which your parents, siblings, extended family, and friends acted
and reacted, you will be able to see how your Trust Factor—
the four expectations for trust outlined in Chapter 1 (You Will
Be There; This Will Last; You Will Be Honest; and You Will
Protect Me)—took shape.

For example, you may think that your parents were old-fashioned and overly strict with you while you were growing up. By trying to protect you, they may have failed to allow you to make some of your own choices and to learn from your mistakes. As an adult, you may waffle when confronted with decision, because you lack confidence in your own judgment.

The lesson here is: Before you can begin to trust others, you first need to understand yourself. To think more clearly about trust in your own life, take a few minutes to consider the following questions. By answering each one honestly, you will illuminate events, circumstances, and patterns of behavior of which you may not be fully aware. Then you will be able to understand the impact they had on your concept of trust in others, as well as your ability to trust your own judgment.

- Were your parents happily married? If they were separated or divorced, how old were you when the marriage fell apart?
- Did either of your parents struggle with alcohol or substance abuse?
- Were your relationships with your siblings friendly and loving? Did you fight a lot as children? What are your relationships with your siblings now?
- In general, how did your parents handle anger? Did they sulk and fume, or scream and throw things?
- Did your parents accept you for who you were, or did you sense that you were never good enough in their eyes?
- Did your parents allow you to make your own decisions? Did they support your choices?
- Could you talk freely with your parents? In general, did

family members speak their mind, or did they subscribe
to the belief that people should keep their personal
thoughts and feelings to themselves?

- Are you extroverted or introverted? Did you have a lot
of friends when you were growing up, or were you a
loner?

- In general, would you describe your parents as
optimistic and trusting? Or were they suspicious and
mistrustful of other people's intentions? Did they exude
a sense of satisfaction with their lives, or did they give
you the impression that the grass was greener on the
other side?

- When you are in a new situation, do you find it easy or
difficult to talk to others? Do you enjoy traveling to
new places and meeting new people?

As I explained in Chapter 1, by looking back on the past you
can shine a light on the present. The nature of your parents'
marriage, the family in which you grew up, and the many ways
all the significant people in your life related to one another
have a dramatic, long-lasting effect on your ability to trust. The
feelings of abandonment you may have felt if your parents divorced or separated when you were young, as well as your anxiety if a close relative struggled with alcohol abuse, can carry
over into your present-day relationships and make you vulnerable to betrayal. Similarly, the nature of your relationship with
your siblings affects your self-esteem as well as the kind of people you bring into your life. Highly competitive sibling relations may cause you to re-create rivalrous relationships today.
At the same time, if people in your past acted and reacted un-
predictably—and you never knew when an angry outburst

would occur—you may shy away from intimacy and be reluctant to place your trust in another. Finally, if you felt you never measured up in your parents' eyes, you may have the need for constant approval and will seek out people who give it to you. This all affects whether you are suspicious, shy, or at ease in the company of strangers. Use these questions to shape your self-awareness.

2. Unearth Your Hidden Agenda

As discussed in Chapter 1, four key expectations make up your Trust Factor—and each means something different to different people. They also influence how you feel about yourself, as well as how you act and react to others.

The lesson here is: Though you may be unaware of them, your harbor specific hopes, beliefs, and requirements regarding each of your relationships. In order to trust again, you must understand your own agenda. What, exactly, do these expectations mean to you? Study each one: You Will Be There; This Will Last; You Will Be Honest; You Will Protect Me. Then, take four sheets of paper and write each expectation across the top. Now, list specific examples of what you look for when you think about each one—either in general, or in relation to a specific person.

For example, under the expectation You Will Be There, you may have written about your husband:

"I expect you to listen when I have a problem at work, even though I've said the same thing ten times."

For a boyfriend, you may have written:

"I expect you to call me often."

Under the heading This Will Last, you may have written:
"No matter what you do, I will always love you."
"I expect you to show me the same love and affection all the time."

Under the heading You Will Be Honest, you may have written:
"I expect you to talk to me first before doing anything that affects me."
"I expect that you won't lie to me when I confront you."

Under the heading You Will Protect Me, you may have written:
"I expect you to hold in confidence the things I tell you."
"I expect that you won't use against me what I tell you."

Figure out which expectations predominate for you and ask yourself whether they are reasonable. Be prepared to scale them down so that they are realistic and are tailored to the particular person with whom you are involved.

For example, if the expectation You Will Be There rules your life, think about whether you may be looking for unlimited attention and involvement; that is, that someone you trust listen to you whenever you need to talk. This may translate into a need for repeated phone calls, or daily or weekly visits, which may not be realistic in light of the other person's needs and personal constraints. Conflict may erupt when two people do not share similar priorities and expectations yet assume that they do. You'll be happier if you shape your expectations realistically. If a friend listens to you complain about your worries on the job once or twice, accept the fact that she cares about your welfare, and don't demand that she prove it to you over and over again.

If you're guided by the expectation This Will Last, consider whether your need for security has locked you into a negative relationship guaranteed to bring you a string of disappointments. See whether you accept and tolerate repeated hurtful behaviors to make the relationship last. Are you willing to put your emotional well-being at risk? If not, then scale down the expectation to: This will last only if you are respectful and honest with me. If you continue to lie, it will not last.

If the belief that You Will Be Honest rules your life, ask yourself how often people fail to check things out with you before acting. If you confront them over their betrayal, and they deny wrongdoing, you must begin to reshape your relationship.

Then, too, if You Will Protect Me is guiding your Trust Factor, don't mistake the sharing of intimacy with security. Safeguard what you share in every relationship so that you don't leave yourself open to betrayal.

3. *Move from Blind Trust to Seeing the Light*

One reason people trust blindly is that they're stuck in one or more of the Trust Sandtraps discussed in Chapter 2. There are elements of truth in each of these sandtraps, but when they become guiding principles, you may not see a way out of emotionally or physically damaging relationships.

The lesson here is: Your hope for what a relationship could be may be blinding you to what it really is. You must realistically assess which sandtrap is preventing you from trusting your own judgment. To do that, take this short quiz:

- Are you easily talked into doing something you don't want to do?
- Do you feel guilty when you doubt or mistrust somebody?
- Are you quick to base your trust on someone's appearance, especially if she is attractive?
- Are you easily flattered by what people tell you, and apt to believe that what they say is true?
- Do you readily believe what someone says because you admire him?
- Do you feel insecure about your own opinions and rely on others to make decisions for you?

A *yes* answer to three or more of these questions means that you fit the profile of someone who is likely to trust blindly. *To get out of the sandtraps:*

- Push for certainty when dealing with others, rather than always giving them the benefit of the doubt. Don't chalk things up to coincidence. Confront people—over and over—until you have enough facts to formulate your own truth. Many people think that confronting someone once is enough. Sometimes it's just the beginning.
- Consider how a person responds when you do confront him. Does he acknowledge his untrustworthy behavior and promise to change? Or does he excuse and/or justify his hurtful actions?
- Look for consistent behavior. The most significant action is someone's following through on what she promises to do. Don't accept what she says at face value to avoid facing the truth. Instead, think about the concrete ways she works to maintain your confidence.
- Base your trust on how you feel when you are with a person: Whether he makes you feel respected, valued, belittled, or ignored. Be wary of the occasional nice gesture—an invitation to dinner; a bouquet of flowers—since it can cloud your vision. Distinguish between the random nice gesture that is convenient for someone but is often self-serving—and the kind of trustworthy behavior that is tailored to your needs.

4. Examine the Role You Played in the Betrayal

When you're smarting from the pain of broken trust, it can be difficult to acknowledge that you played any part in what occurred. Nevertheless, in most cases, victims do play a small role in their own betrayal. Accepting this is a key step in the healing process. *The lesson here is:* Many people are unaware of the subtle messages they may be sending, messages that affect the way other people perceive them. For example, perhaps you are, or have been in the past, so sensitive and tense that a partner or friend may be reluctant to express any negative feelings for fear of triggering your angry response. You need to re-evaluate your actions and imagine how they may be interpreted by others. How can you do this? Answer the following questions honestly:

- Do you convey to friends or lovers a sense of helplessness or neediness? Do you give the impression that you are willing to let them control your life and make decisions for you?
- Are you too reactive? Do others avoid talking to you because they are afraid you'll explode in anger?
- Conversely, do you come across as so agreeable and accommodating that people believe they can get away with anything?
- Have you ever tried to justify your own hurtful actions to others?

If you've answered *yes* to these questions, you may have played a greater role in the betrayal than you realize. To understand how, think about the nature of the betrayal and whether it was an unaware, a couldn't-help-it, or a deliberate betrayal. (Check back to Chapter 3 to refresh your memory.) Once you've determined the other person's motivation, you may discover, for example, that your inability to make up your mind gave him the impression that you wanted him to make decisions for you. If that's the case, learn from your experience that you need to take more responsibility for your own decision-making.

If what happened to you was a couldn't-help-it betrayal, one in which the person could justify that he was looking out for your best interests, you may be giving him and others too much access to, and control over, your life. He may feel he has a right to do what he does. If your betrayer knew what he was doing but couldn't talk to you about it, perhaps you are more reactive or close-minded than you want to admit. If it was a deliberate betrayal, consider whether you did anything—even a long time ago—that may have provoked your betrayer to retaliate.

5. Rebuild Your Self-esteem

Self-esteem is the feeling of pride, confidence, and self-worth that comes from living up to your own expectations. Everyone sets expectations for herself regarding what she wants to achieve as well as how she thinks she should look, behave, and respond. Sometimes, you fall short of these expectations, but if self-esteem is in place, you can be sure that you won't fall apart, at least for too long. Since the heaviest impact of betrayal is the demolition job it does on self-esteem, reclaiming yours after trust is broken is usually the most difficult task you will face.

Remember, too, that genuinely confident people don't have all their self-esteem tied to one area of their lives. When your life is balanced and diversified—by family, friends, work, and avocations—a blow in one area won't knock you down forever. Sure, you may be angry, hurt, or jealous, but such negative feelings won't stick around for long. Self-esteem gives you the knowledge that you will survive betrayal, even though a particular relationship may not.

The lesson here is: Unless you feel self-worth, you cannot trust yourself—or anyone else. When you are confident, you acknowledge your strengths and weaknesses and set realistic goals for yourself and others. However, if you are unable to see your own merits; if you think your achievements are the result only of somebody's liking you or giving you a break; if you feel good only if you are doing for others, often putting your own needs last—you may lose your emotional compass. Instead of trusting yourself for direction, you turn to others and become dependent on their approval to feel good about yourself.

The following exercises can help you zero in on what you need to do to feel good about yourself:

SELF-ESTEEM BOOSTER #1

Balance the good with the bad.

On a sheet of paper, make three columns: one headed *Qualities I Know I Have,* another *Qualities I Lack,* and the third, *Qualities I Aspire to Have.* Now, describe yourself under each heading. Many people pale in the face of their limitations and are unable to see any good in themselves at all. The simple act of writing down your strengths and weaknesses can put them into perspective and help you balance any shame or embarrassment these weaknesses may cause you. What's more, if you fear that others will one day discover that you are not as intelligent, competent, or worthy as you appear to be or as they think you are—the so-called imposter syndrome—this exercise will reinforce your positive attributes.

SELF-ESTEEM BOOSTER #2

Determine what your self-expectations and assumptions are based on: your own past experiences? What others tell you about yourself? What you *think* others think of you?

To do this, make a list of your trigger points—those weaknesses you consistently use to condemn yourself—and name the person who originally criticized you for these faults.

For instance, your mother or father may have called you selfish or lazy. Early labels stick, and although you have worked hard at school or on your job, you may still hear a nagging voice telling you that, despite your achievements, you should be doing even more. No matter what you've accomplished, deep down you're convinced you *are* lazy. What's more, any time a friend or lover implies that you are, he hits that trigger, wounds you deeply, and quickly puts you on the defensive.

Now, look over the list of your trigger points and challenge them one at a time. Are you really lazy? What could you do to feel more industrious? Instead of having the ambiguous notion that you must be working all the time, set small, specific goals that you can meet. For example, if you just went back to work after having a baby, and you berate yourself for not keeping the house as clean as you'd like, decide what you can do to improve the situation and begin to feel good about it. You may decide you need to vacuum only every other week, instead of every other day, until the baby is on a more regular schedule. Or you may decide that simply clearing the living room floor of toys before you go to bed is good enough. The point of this self-esteem booster is for *you* to determine your personal equation for what feels sufficient. Unless you set these clear guidelines, no matter how much you do, you will still feel you haven't done enough. And that translates into "I'm not good enough."

SELF-ESTEEM BOOSTER #3

Identify your potential betrayers.

Ask yourself if your emotional needs cause you to gravitate toward a particular type of person—a Rival, an Admirer, or a User. (Refer to Chapters 4, 5, and 6 for more information.) Once you determine this, you can zero in on the specific self-esteem needs you may be attempting to fill in the relationship and begin to seek out people who enhance, rather than negate, your self-esteem.

For instance, if you are often trapped in rivalrous relationships, you may be struggling with unresolved parent or sibling issues. Perhaps you're more competitive than you realize, and set up rivalrous situations to enhance your self-esteem by proving that you're the best. If so, instead of feverishly trying to outdo others, prove yourself worthy by competing against your own victories to motivate yourself toward your personal best. Stop trying to measure your worth by using other people's achievements as a yardstick.

If you gravitate toward an Admirer, you may feel that your life is incomplete and look to raise your self-esteem by basking in her admiration. If this is the case, you need to develop a new network of friends or refocus your energies on a new hobby. This way, your sense of well-being will stem from things you accomplish rather than things other people do or the things you do for them. Also, instead of seeking praise and admiration from others, learn to give yourself approval for the things you do to take care of yourself.

If you have a pattern of Users in your life, be aware that you may be emotionally powerless and vulnerable—due, perhaps, to a family illness or death or the loss of a job. By always giving to another person, you may experience a temporary, and false, sense of strength and control. Instead, make sure that every relationship you enter is balanced, and that your needs are made known and attended to from the start. Distinguish between love and lust. Sexual desire can be intense, but it can cool quickly. Make sure you feel desired for who you are as a person. Also, if you are ambivalent about the person or the relationship, be careful about talking over the pros and cons with others. Keep your own counsel so that you are not negatively swayed by their opinions. Finally, set limits so that you do not overextend yourself. To learn how to do that, see Lesson 7, below.

SELF-ESTEEM BOOSTER #4

Banish self-blame. Negative talk about yourself quickly destroys self-esteem. If you find yourself thinking, "I'm just lucky," and dismiss your talents and abilities, remind yourself that, though luck is a combination of being in the right place at the right time, you must have worked hard to get to that spot. Luck demands ambition, perseverance, and determination; it doesn't just happen. Many people think that film stars have "overnight success," forgetting the years of low-paying, bit parts in B-movies they had to endure before they "suddenly" appeared in *People* magazine.

6. *Learn to Spot a Toxic Friendship*

Unfulfilling friendships can be just as toxic to your emotional well-being as an unhappy childhood or a bad marriage. However, it can be very difficult to spot the signs of a poisoned friendship. You may feel belittled, angry, edgy, or frustrated, yet unable to put your finger on why this relationship is eating away at your self-esteem. That's because someone may have betrayed you in small ways, which you dismissed or rationalized on the surface, though you still harbor a deep hurt.

The lesson here is: Learn to trust your instincts and your judgment. Asking yourself who your real friends are takes more intellectual and emotional honesty than most people realize. Be sure you choose friendships that are mutual and balanced when it comes to giving and receiving.

To help focus your thoughts, grab a piece of paper and write down, honestly, your answers to the following questions.

- Do you spend your free time doing favors or running errands for this person?
- Are marathon phone conversations one-sided—always in her favor—as you help her solve her problems?
- Do you often volunteer to lend this person your possessions—clothing, money, a computer—and feel reluctant to ask for them back?
- Does this person present the ideas or remarks you make

in confidence as his own clever ideas or witty perceptions?

- Do you share your fears and vulnerabilities, only to find them publicly revealed, in a joking manner?
- Do you willingly include this friend when you get together with others, only to discover that she is ingratiating herself with your old friends, making her own plans with them, and cutting you out?

If you answered *yes* to any of these questions, you may be in a relationship that either is, or will soon be, detrimental to your well-being. Play detective and look for clues. If other people tell you to watch out, pay attention to whether their comments confirm your own fears or doubts. Also, consider what this friendship really means to you. Perhaps it provides support, companionship, or a sense of safety. Think about other ways to get what you need from the friendship. One option may be to limit your relationship rather than severing it completely. Instead of having an all-purpose friend-for-life, for instance, confine your time to a specific activity—say, biking or going to an exercise class. You can cut back the amount of time you spend together; instead of having dinner, meet for breakfast before work. Other limits may also be necessary to redefine the relationship. If so, determine what they are—Lesson 7—and implement them.

7. Set Limits That Make Sense

Make a commitment to resolve episodes of broken trust in each relationship, without mud-slinging or martyrdom, *when they occur.* Being direct and setting limits in the face of hurtful behavior is the most important step you can take to protect yourself. Your verbal declaration that "I count and I won't take it anymore" frees you from the simmering hostility that can erode trust.

The lesson here is: Any relationship that cannot tolerate a re-definition of the rules, so that there is room for both of you, may not be worth saving. Remember, the key to setting limits is not to get the other person to change. Rather, it is for you to make a change; it is an opportunity to make your Trust Factor practical and applicable to all your relationships.

You can set boundaries for yourself and others by determining your Trust Bottom Line. Four elements make up your Trust Bottom Line:

- Your expectations of the other person in a relationship.
- What behavior you can accept and ultimately forgive and what actions you can never condone.
- How much disappointment you will tolerate in the relationship.
- The new actions you will take if the betraying behavior occurs again.

When one aggrieved wife thought about this, she realized she could never trust her husband to be on time or to accomplish any of the things on his to-do list. For years, she had felt angry and betrayed. Once she determined her Trust Bottom Line, she realized she could accept her husband's failure to be there for her when it came to his to-do list—such as picking up the dry cleaning or even remembering a dinner date—but she could not tolerate his procrastination regarding major repairs around the house. She learned to say, "Danny, the window in the den is leaking." If he replied, "I'll fix it this weekend," she'd say, "Fine, but if it's not fixed by then, on Monday morning I'm calling a repairman." Then she would follow through with her plan. She no longer felt enraged and helpless—and the window got fixed either way.

You can adopt this technique in other situations, too. If your husband consistently embarrasses you in public, decide now that you will leave a party or a restaurant the moment he begins to belittle you. Tell him: "I won't accept your embarrassing behavior, and if it happens again, this is what I'm going to do." If a friend always keeps you waiting when you make a date, let her know that the next time it happens, you will wait fifteen minutes, not a moment longer, and then leave if she hasn't shown up.

Another reason to set limits is to make sure you don't overextend your emotional resources. Most likely you've been selfless for too long. Stop being a yesman and learn to say, "I'd like to help you out, but I'm just not able to do that now."

Remember that, though you may be devastated by broken trust, you don't have to feel that way forever. Make a decision now to trust people again, and plant both feet firmly on the side of commitment. Yes, you will have to take an emotional risk, but in the end you will gain the confidence and strength that come from a truly intimate, trusting relationship.

THE TEN COMMANDMENTS OF TRUST

When I asked men and women who have attended my workshops on relationships to fill out questionnaires about what they would do differently in the wake of betrayal, their comments proved fresh and psychologically valid. Here's what they reported:

1. I will express my feelings and verbalize my needs more often and early on.

2. I will set boundaries.

3. I will trust my own judgment more.

4. I will be more suspicious and not take people at their word without objective, corroborating proof.

5. I will ask more questions and check things out in my relationships.

6. I will move more slowly in a relationship so that I can protect myself more.

7. I will deal with what is, instead of wishing for what might be.

8. I will walk away earlier from a relationship when my needs aren't being met.

9. I will not blame myself for everything that goes wrong.

10. I will not sabotage a relationship with temper tantrums.

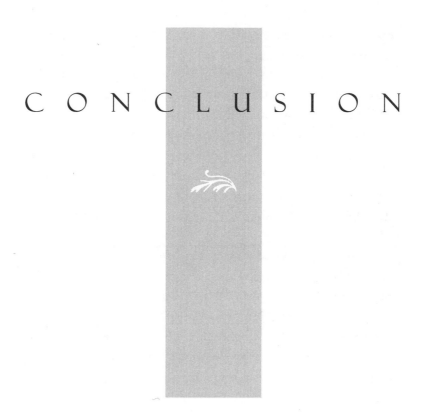

CONCLUSION

Trust is a basic human need, essential for our existence. Without trust, we have no meaningful connections, no intimacy, no anchor. On a more mundane level, trust allows us to live our life in a normal fashion. We trust that the restaurant where we go for lunch will not serve contaminated food, that the taxi driver taking us to the airport will not get into an accident, that the cars on the road will stop at the intersection when the light turns red so that we can cross safely.

When someone you expect to be there for you lets you down, the sense of betrayal is profound and devastating. The protective fabric of trust that you weave from your earliest childhood experiences with parents, siblings, and friends begins to fray—and you are left feeling alone, frightened, unsafe. "How could I let this happen?" you wonder. "If only I'd known better," you lament. Fundamentally, what you want to know is: "How can you ever learn to trust again?"

Every day, people make decisions to trust too little or too much, based on faulty evidence—because someone looks trustworthy, because we want to trust, or because a person assures us that he can be trusted. Trust is vital to us, yet people often slip easily, often blindly, into situations that lead directly to betrayal.

Some of the world's most renowned theoreticians have tried for years to examine the intriguing nature of trust, but until now, no one has taken the psychological theories and applied them in a meaningful way to the hundreds of trust decisions people make in their daily lives. That's precisely what I've tried to do in this book. By examining trust and betrayal from every angle, I have painted a picture of trust that you not only can recognize but also can dismantle, as you examine, piece by piece, the expectations, values, and beliefs that guide your life and your interactions with others.

In Chapter 1, you looked at the roots of trust—the Trust Factor each person has that helps him formulate his mental checklist of who is trustworthy and who isn't. In reading Chapter 2, you learned to zero in on the sandtraps that many people unwittingly slide into when they base a person's trustworthiness on superficial signs rather than on meaningful actions. By recognizing these common traps, and by understanding the key reasons that compel people to betray a trust, discussed in Chapter 3, you will be able to focus on where trust begins, and ends, for you.

Conclusion

You may not have realized that there was a pattern to your trust in several respects: that the people in whom you place your trust, as well as the way you respond to them, may have striking similarities. Then, too, there may be a pattern to the betrayals you have experienced, whether they happened with family members, friends, or colleagues. In Chapters 4, 5, and 6, you peeled away the façade of the three types of people—the Rival, the Admirer, the User—most likely to betray a trust. Now that you know how to spot your betrayers and the reasons you may be vulnerable to them, you can avoid hurtful situations and heal more quickly from those you can't.

Finally, you explored the aftermath of broken trust. In Chapter 7, you saw that seeking revenge as your only solace can hurt you more than it hurts your betrayer. On reading Chapters 8 and 9, you learned the talk tactics to confront a betrayer and to determine whether you should accept an apology and forgive, or end a relationship entirely. What's more, if you were the one to betray, you can now apologize in a heartfelt and sincere way. The lessons learned there, as well as in Chapter 10, allow you to set limits for yourself and others in every relationship.

Indeed, as you begin to trust yourself again, with clarity and assurance, in time you will feel secure enough to take the risk of trusting others. To survive, trust must be shared. I trust that now you can begin.

BIBLIOGRAPHY

Anthony, E. James, M.D., and Therese Benedek, eds. *Parenthood: Its Psychology and Psychopathology.* Boston, Little, Brown & Co., 1970.

Barker, Robert L. *Surviving Jealous Relationships: The Green-Eyed Marriage.* New York, The Free Press, 1987.

Bok, Sissela. *Lying: Moral Choice in Public and Private Life.* New York, Pantheon, 1978.

Casargian, Robin. *Forgiveness: A Bold Choice for a Peaceful Heart.* New York, Bantam Books, 1992.

Coleman, Paul W. *The Forgiving Marriage: Resolving Anger and Resentment and Rediscovering Each Other.* Chicago, Contemporary Books, 1989.

Daniels, Marvin. "Pathological Vindictiveness and the Vindictive Character," *Psychoanalytic Review,* vol. 56, 1969.

Diagnostic and Statistical Manual of Mental Disorders. 4th ed. Washington, D.C., American Psychiatric Association, 1994.

Bibliography

Edward, Joyce, Nathene Ruskin, and Patsy Turrini. *Separation Individuation Theory and Application.* 2nd ed. New York, Gardner Press, 1991.

Ekman, Paul. *Telling Lies.* New York, W. W. Norton, 1992.

Gabriel, Martha A., and Gail W. Monaco. "Getting Even: Clinical Considerations of Adaptive and Maladaptive Vengeance," *Clinical Social Work Journal,* vol. 22, no. 2, Summer 1994.

Goldberg, Arnold. "Psychotherapy of Narcissistic Injuries," *Archives of General Psychiatry,* vol. 28, May 1973.

Greer, Jane. *Twinship and Marital Adjustments.* Ann Arbor, Mich., University Microfilms International, 1985.

Greer, Jane, with Edward Myers. *Adult Sibling Rivalry: Understanding the Legacy of Childhood.* New York, Crown, 1992.

Hinsie, Leland E., and Robert J. Campbell. *Psychiatric Dictionary.* 4th ed. New York, Oxford University Press, 1970.

Horney, Karen. "The Value of Vindictiveness," *American Journal of Psychoanalysis,* vol 8–13, 1948–53.

Keyishian, Harry. "Karen Horney on the Value of Vindictiveness," *American Journal of Psychoanalysis,* vol. 42, 1982.

Kirman, William. "Revenge and Accommodation in the Family," *Modern Psychoanalysis,* vol. 14 (1), 1989.

Bibliography

Klein, Charles. *How to Forgive When You Can't Forget: Healing Our Personal Relationships.* Bellmore, N.Y., Leibling Press, 1995.

Mahler, Margaret S., Fred Pine, and Anni Bergman. *The Psychological Birth of the Human Infant.* New York, Basic Books, 1975.

Nelson, Judith. "Varieties of Narcissistically Vulnerable Couples: Dynamics and Practice Implications," *Clinical Social Work,* vol. 23, no. 1, Spring 1995.

Rothstein, Arnold. *The Narcissistic Pursuit of Perfection.* New York, International Universities Press, 1980.

Stolorow, Robert D., and Frank M. Lachman. *Psychoanalysis of Developmental Arrests: Theory and Treatment.* New York, International Universities Press, 1983.

Turner, Francis F. *Adult Psychopathology.* New York, The Free Press, 1984.

Webster's New World Dictionary. 2nd college edition. Antioch, Tenn., The World Publishing Company, 1970.

White, Marjorie Taggart, and Marcella Bakur Weiner. *The Theory and Practice of Self Psychology.* New York, Brunner-Mazel, 1986.